AF600431

THE CATHOLIC UNIVERSITY OF AMERICA
CANON LAW STUDIES
No. 257

Legislative Powers of the Provincial Council

A HISTORICAL SYNOPSIS AND A COMMENTARY

By the

REV. FRANCIS JOSEPH MURPHY, A.B., J.C.L.
Priest of the Diocese of Raleigh

A DISSERTATION

Submitted to the Faculty of the School of Canon Law of the Catholic University of America in Partial Fulfillment of the Requirements for the Degree of Doctor of Canon Law

THE CATHOLIC UNIVERSITY OF AMERICA PRESS
WASHINGTON, D. C.
1947

Nihil Obstat:
Ludovicus Motry, S.T.D., J.C.D.,
Censor Deputatus.
Washingtonii, die 23 maii, 1947.
Imprimatur:
✠ Vincentius S. Waters, D.D.,
Episcopus Raleighiensis.
Raleigh, die 23 maii, 1947.

COPYRIGHT, 1948,
THE CATHOLIC UNIVERSITY OF AMERICA PRESS, INC.

Printed by
The Paulist Press
401 West 59th Street
New York 19, N. Y.
51

TO MARY

MOTHER OF GOOD COUNSEL

TABLE OF CONTENTS

CHAPTER II

PART II

CANONICAL COMMENTARY

CHAPTER III

CHAPTER IV

CHAPTER VII

FOREWORD

As a permanent world-wide society which tends to the salvation of immortal souls, the Church governs her members by means of laws. That the laws of the Church are holy, since God sanctions them and blesses their observance, is a conviction that is rooted in our Faith. But as our knowledge increases concerning the nature and practical application of the Church's laws, our appreciation deepens for the wisdom and tender solicitude which she breathes into those laws.

Such is the law which requires the celebration of provincial councils. Provincial councils may be termed guardians of the common law of the Church, for they play a specific part in the maintaining of the uniform observance of the common law. As localities differ, so must provincial laws. But if provinces are bereft of apt and timely local legislation, the great good of unity, in which there is strength, suffers, ecclesiastical discipline is impaired, and the observance of the common law is weakened.

From the first centuries of her existence unto the present day, the constant legislation of the Church concerning the celebration of provincial councils reflects their importance. How, in the face of this legislation, councils could have been neglected presents a challenge and bears the marks of an interesting historical question.

Many aspects of the provincial councils are of commanding interest, for these councils stand as monuments of the living Church, and their history embraces a wide span of years and climes and events. But for the compass and purpose of this work, primarily selected were those factors which seemed to throw greater light upon, and to be more closely connected with, the provincial council as it exists today in its legislative function.

In the canonical commentary an attempt was made to establish the *raison d'être* of the provincial council as a legislative agency, chiefly through an investigation of canons 283 to 291. Provincial conciliar legislation embraces a very wide field and comes into contact with the general law of the Church in many interesting ways.

Moreover, commentators upon the pertinent canons of the present study are few, and not infrequently in the course of the dissertation the writer was confronted with a *lacuna legis* which apparently had not been explored by authors. But, despite the breadth of the subject, for the sake of the reader's interest and convenience of reference it was deemed better to consider the general aspects of the council as a legislative agency according to the pattern of the Code, rather than to treat a more restricted phase of the subject. The intrinsic constitution and limitations of the provincial council, its particular objective, scope and methods of legislating, its convocation and celebration, and the force of its conciliar decrees are analyzed in successive chapters.

The writer takes this occasion to express his sincere gratitude to His Excellency, the Most Reverend Vincent S. Waters, Bishop of Raleigh, and to His Excellency, the Most Reverend Eugene J. McGuinness, former Bishop of Raleigh, for the opportunity to pursue advanced studies at the Catholic University of America. Sincere thanks are also expressed to friends at the University and elsewhere, especially to the members of the Faculty of the School of Canon Law, for their generous assistance and encouragement, and to all who in any way aided in the completion of this dissertation.

PART ONE

HISTORICAL SYNOPSIS

INTRODUCTION

ARTICLE 1. NATURE OF THE PROVINCIAL COUNCIL

THE object of this study is the provincial council, as distinguished from plenary (embracing more than one province) and ecumenical (general) councils. A provincial council is the legitimate assembly of the bishops of an ecclesiastical province for the purpose of deliberating upon and decreeing for the ecclesiastical needs of that province.[1]

Among ecclesiastical authors, the word "council" is found for the first time in Tertullian (ca. 160-ca. 230).[2] He praises the holding of councils, which he describes as a source of edification.[3] Instead of "council," the original Greek term "synod" (σύνοδος) appears regularly in early usage in the Church, and thus it is found among the Apostolic canons.[4] For the sake of uniformity, however, the term "council" will be employed exclusively throughout this dissertation, except when reference is made to a diocesan synod.

[1] Wernz, *Ius Decretalium* (2. ed., 6 vols., Romae et Prati, 1905-1913), II, n. 843 (hereafter cited as Wernz); Bouix, *De Concilio Provinciali* (3. ed., Parisiis, 1884), p. 1; cf. Panormitanus (Nicolaus de Tudeschis), *Commentaria in Quinque Decretalium Libros* (7 vols. in 5, Venetiis, 1588), Lib. V, tit. 1, *de accusationibus, inquisitionibus et denunciationibus,* cap. 25, n. 1. A provincial council possesses legislative, administrative, coactive and judiciary powers. Cf. *infra,* Chapter III, Article 1, pp. 29-31.

[2] *De Ieiunio,* cap. 13: "Aguntur praeterea per Graecias illa certis in locis concilia ex universis ecclesiis. . ."—*Corpus Scriptorum Ecclesiasticorum Latinorum* (68 vols., incomplete, Vindobonae, 1866—), XX, pars I, 292 (hereafter cited as *CSEL*). It may be observed that Tertullian was trained in law and that *concilium* was a term of Roman administrative law.

[3] *Loc. cit.*: "Et hoc quam dignum fide auspicante congregari undique ad Christum."

[4] Can. 36—Bruns, *Canones Apostolorum et Conciliorum Saeculorum IV-VII* (2 vols., Berolini, 1839), I, 6. (Hereafter cited as Bruns.)

Article 2. Early Councils

It was of Apostolic tradition, according to Baronius (1538-1607), that there should be a general assembly of the bishops on the occasion of controversies concerning the Faith, or whenever very difficult matters arose for consideration.[5] To check the rise of Montanism, councils were held in the middle of the second century.[6] So, too, councils met the issues inherent in the Paschal controversy and the heresy of Paul of Samosata.[7] That provincial councils were held regularly in the third century may be deduced from a letter of Firmilian, Bishop of Caesarea of Cappadocia (+268), in which he writes to St. Cyprian (+258).[8] The early fourth century saw the Peace of Constantine and the end of persecutions against the Church. The Church's newly found freedom and the favoring action of the emperors gave new impetus to conciliar activity.

[5] *Annales Ecclesiastici* (ed. A. Theiner, 37 vols., Vols. I-XXVIII, Barri-Ducis, 1864-1875; Vols. XXIX-XXXVII, Parisiis, 1876-1883), II, pp. 351, 352, n. 19.

[6] Eusebius, *Historia Ecclesiastica*, Lib. V, n. 19—*Die Griechischen Christlichen Schriftsteller der ersten drei Jahrhunderte*—(Eusebius, 7 vols. in 10, Vol. II, pars I [1903], pars II [1908], Leipzig, 1903-1908), II, pars I, p. 464, n. 16 (hereafter cited as *GCS*); Ceillier, *Histoire Générale des Auteurs Sacrés et Ecclésiastiques* (14 vols. in 17, Paris, 1858-1869), II, 537 (hereafter cited as Ceillier); Hafele-Leclercq, *Histoire des Conciles* (nouvelle traduction française, 10 vols. in 19, Paris, 1907-1938), I, 3, 24 (hereafter cited as Hafele-Leclercq).

[7] Ceillier, II, 541; Eusebius, *Historia Ecclesiastica*, Lib. VII, nn. 27, 28—*GCS*, II, pars II, 702, 704.

[8] Thomassinus, *Vetus et Nova Ecclesiae Disciplina circa Beneficia et Beneficiarios* (3 partes in 10 vols., ed. postrema cum Parisieni accuratissime collata, Magontiaci, 1787), Pars II, lib. III, cap. 45, nn. 2, 3 (hereafter cited as Thomassinus); cf. Migne, *Patrologiae Cursus Completus* (*Series Latina*, 221 vols., Parisiis, 1844-1864), IV, 413 (hereafter cited as *MPL*).

CHAPTER I

LEGISLATION BEFORE THE COUNCIL OF TRENT

Article 1. Frequency of Celebrating the Provincial Council

A. The Law and the Extent of Its Observance

1. From the I Council of Nicaea to the Sixth Century

Such importance had the provincial council attained by the year 325 that the obligation of holding provincial councils twice each year was decreed by the I Ecumenical Council of Nicaea in its fifth canon.[1] This canon further prescribed that the first of these councils was to be held before Lent, and the second of them in the autumn. Less than twenty years later this law regarding the semi-annual celebration of councils was restated by the Council of Antioch (341).[2] But the decree of the Council of Antioch specified that one of the councils should take place in the fourth week after Easter, and the second on the Ides (or fifteenth) of October. While the text of this canon (originally in Greek) would place the Ides on the tenth of October, the *glossa ordinaria* explains that the Greek months were not altogether in harmony with the Latin calendar.[3] Moreover, the

[1] Can. 5—Bruns, I, 15; Hardouin, *Acta Conciliorum et Epistolae Decretales* (12 vols., Parisiis, 1714-1715), I, 326; c. 3, D. XVIII.

[2] Can. 20—Bruns, I, 85; c. 4, D. XVIII; Turner, *Ecclesiae Occidentalis Monumenta Iuris Antiquissima, Canonum et Conciliorum Graecorum Interpretationes Latinae* (2 vols. in 6, Oxonii: E. Typographia Clarendoniana, Vol. II, pars II, 1913), II, pars II, 290-293. For the recently advanced opinion that the date of the Council of Antioch followed shortly after that of the I Council of Nicaea (325), cf. Van Hove, *Commentarium Lovaniense in Codicem Iuris Canonici,* Vol. I, Tom. I, *Prolegomena ad Codicem Iuris Canonici* (2. ed. auctior et emendatior, Mechliniae et Romae: Dessain, 1945), p. 143.

[3] *Glossa ordinaria,* c. 4, D. XVIII, ad v. *decimus.*

expression "on the Ides of October" is aptly explained as including the days which were calculated from the Ides, namely, the eighth to the fifteenth of October inclusive.[4] Thus there was a more exact specification of the time for the fall provincial council, in contrast to the phrase *"circa tempus autumni,"* as used by the Council of Nicaea.[5] It is to be noted that this specifying of the exact time points to a practical emphasis on, and facilitation of, the regular celebration of councils. The importance of the law of frequent celebration may be inferred also from its reiteration in later canonical enactments, as included in canons two, six, seven and fifteen of the eighteenth Distinction of Gratian, and in the further specification of details of the law, as given by most of the remaining canons of this eighteenth Distinction.[6]

The insistence upon the law of the semi-annual celebration of provincial councils is indicative of its importance. But the frequent repetition of this law also suggests, perhaps, that councils were not being held with due regularity. Thus, in the year 446, Pope St. Leo I, in a letter to Anastasius, Bishop of Thessalonica, urged the observ-

[4] *Glossa ordinaria,* c. 4, D. XVIII, ad v. *Idibus.*

[5] The I Council of Nicaea had indicated with a quite general expression that the provincial council should be held "ante dies quadragesimae"—before the season of Lent. The Council of Antioch appointed the time of this council more determinately, namely, that it should be celebrated in the week which fell mid-way between Easter and Pentecost Sundays. In explanation of the difference existing between these decrees of the Councils of Nicaea and Antioch, twelfth century commentators pointed out that the authority of the Council of Nicaea, as an Ecumenical Council, outweighed that of the Council of Antioch, and so was to be preferred. An alternate explanation was that the exact time for holding the council could vary with the custom of the place. Cf. Rufinus (who wrote c. aa. 1157-1159), *Summa Decretorum* (ed. H. Singer, Paderborn, 1902), D. XVIII.

[6] Cf. cc. 5, 6, 10, 12, 13, 14, D. XVIII, which define sanctions for neglect of the law on the part of metropolitans or of suffragan bishops; cc. 10, 13, 14, D. XVIII, which define legitimate causes for absence from the council; c. 9, D. XVIII, which requires a legitimately impeded bishop to send a proxy. (The penalty stated in c. 17, D. XVIII, is directed against failure to call a diocesan synod for the publication of the conciliar decrees.) The sources of the here listed canons will be indicated in the more detailed consideration of the canons in the following pages.

ance of this law.[7] Again, in the year 451, the law was repeated by the Council of Chalcedon, in its nineteenth canon.[8] As late as the year 572, the II Council of Braga declared that provincial councils should be held twice each year.[9]

But the non-observance of this law and the relaxation of the strict rule is perceived in particular legislation of the years 439 [10] and 441.[11] This laxity of observance is given still clearer expression by the Ecumenical Council of Chalcedon (451), which states that the failure to celebrate provincial councils is proved from the fact that many ecclesiastical matters, which need correction, are being neglected.[12] The tenor of this canon is one of sharp disapproval.[13] Particular legislation, shortly before this date, had referred to the troubled condition of the times as an excuse from the rigid enforcement of the semi-annual celebration.[14]

The rise of national councils, which flourished first in Africa as early as the fourth century, with their frequency regulated by legis-

[7] C. 2, D. XVIII—Jaffé, *Regesta Pontificum Romanorum ab condita Ecclesia ad annum post Christum natum MCXCVIII* (2. ed., 2 vols. in 1, Lipsiae, 1885-1888), n. 411. (Hereafter cited as Jaffé.)

[8] Bruns, I, 30; c. 6, D. XVIII.

[9] Can. 18—Bruns, II, 47; c. 15, D. XVIII.

[10] Council of Riez, can. 8: "Si quies temporum erit, bis in anno conventus agant."—Bruns, II, 120.

[11] I Council of Orange, can. 29: ". . . bis in anno pro temporum qualitate difficile est."—Bruns, II, 126.

[12] C. 5, D. XVIII.

[13] Can. 19, Council of Chalcedon (451): "Pervenit ad nostras aures quod in provinciis constituta episcoporum concilia minime celebrentur. Hoc ex eo probatur, quod multae, quae correctione opus habent ecclesiasticae res negligantur. Statuit ergo haec sancta synodus, secundum Patrum regulas bis in anno in unum convenire per singulas provincias episcopos, ubi singula, quae emerserint, corrigantur"—Mansi, *Sacrorum Conciliorum Nova et Amplissima Collectio*, 53 vols. in 60, Paris, Arnhem, Leipzig, 1901-1927), VII, 389, 390 (hereafter cited as Mansi); c. 6, D. XVIII; cf. Bruns, I, 30.

[14] Cann. 8, 10, Council of Riez (439)—Bruns, II, 120, 121; can. 29, I Council of Orange (441)—Bruns, II, 126.

lation.[15] as well as the later development of these councils in France and Spain, was sometimes regarded as overshadowing the need for provincial councils.[16]

2. From the Sixth Century to the Ninth Century

Early in the sixth century there appears a stream of particular legislation approving a change in the frequency of celebration. Instead of twice yearly, provincial councils, according to Frankish canonical legislation, were to be held at least once a year.[17] This legislation found frequent repetition elsewhere in the seventh century also.[18]

Although the II Council of Braga (572) in canon 18 adhered to the ancient rule of holding councils twice a year,[19] the lax observance of the era was reflected in a canon of the II Council of Mâcon, in 585, which enacted that provincial councils should be celebrated every third year. It was clear testimony of the state of decline in the celebration of Frankish councils.[20] The excuse was offered by the III Council of Toledo (589) that a change to annual councils was being made in consideration both of the length of the journeys involved and of the poverty of the Spanish churches.[21]

The neglect regarding the celebration of councils is reflected in a letter written by Pope St. Gregory the Great in the year 590. In

[15] Hinschius, *Das Kirchenrecht der Katholiken und Protestanten in Deutschland* (6 vols., Berlin, 1869-1897), III, 511 (hereafter cited as Hinschius).

[16] Cf. *infra*, p. 7.

[17] Cf., e.g., can. 71, Council of Agde (506)—Bruns, II, 159; can. 2, II Council of Orleans (533)—*Monumenta Germaniae Historica, Legum Sectio III, Concilia* (2 vols. in 4, ed. Maassen, Werminghoff, Bastgen, Hannoverae et Lipsiae, 1893-1924), I, pars I, 62 (hereafter cited as *MGH, Conc.*); Bruns, II, 185; can. 1, III Council of Orleans (538)—*MGH, Conc.*, I, pars I, 73; Bruns, II, 191; can. 37, IV Council of Orleans (541)—*MGH, Conc.*, I, pars I, 95; Bruns, II, 208; can. 23, V Council of Orleans (549)—*MGH, Conc.*, I, pars I, 108; Bruns, II, 225.

[18] Cf. can. 3, IV Council of Toledo (633)—Bruns, I, 222; can. 7, Council of Hereford (673)—Bruns, II, 310; can. 8, Trullan Council (692)—Bruns, I, 40.

[19] Bruns, II, 47; c. 15, D. XVIII.

[20] Can. 20—Bruns, II, 255; Mansi, IX, 957.

[21] Can. 18: ". . . consulta itineris longitudine et paupertate ecclesiarum Hispaniae."—Bruns, I, 217.

this letter the Pope exhorted the Bishops of Sicily to hold a council each year for the needs of the province, for the benefit of the churches, and in consideration of the poor and the oppressed.[22] The same Pope wrote also to the Kings of Gaul with the request that they use their influence to encourage the holding of councils.[23]

In the year 787 came the important legislation of another Ecumenical Council, the II Council of Nicaea. Its sixth canon stated firmly (*"omni excusatione remota"*) that by all means councils were to be held in each province once a year.[24] It was the first ecumenical council to approve the less rigid discipline. This canon takes cognizance of the physical weariness and difficulties of travel attendant upon the celebration of councils, and so moderated the previous law, but reprimanded all non-compliance and refused to countenance weak excuses for any evasion of the law.

From these phrases may be inferred the existing non-observance of the law—a fact which is expressed again explicitly, for ninth century France, by the VI Council of Paris (829).[25] Thomassinus (1619-1695) mentioned that national councils,[26] to which Charlemagne (+814) gave his support and influence, were held with great frequency, and it was felt that the necessity for provincial councils was thereby superseded.[27] But often simultaneous provincial councils took the place of one national council, as, for instance, five in the year 813.[28]

It is not within the present scope to enter into a discussion of the breakdown of the metropolitan's power in the eighth century,[29]

[22] Lib. I, Ep. 1—*Monumenta Germaniae Historica, Gregorii I Papae Registrum Epistolarum* (4 vols., ed. L. M. Hartmann et P. Ewald, *Epistolarum*, Vol. I, pars II, Berolini, 1891), I, pars II, 1, 2.

[23] Thomassinus, Pars II, lib. III, cap. 50, n. 1.

[24] C. 7, D. XVIII; can. 6—Mansi, XIII, 425-428.

[25] Can. 26—Mansi, XIV, 556, 557; *MGH, Conc.*, II, pars II, 628, 629.

[26] E.g., the Councils of Salz (803-804) and of Aix-la-Chapelle (801, 802, 809, 811)—Hefele-Leclercq, III, 1123, 1117, 1129, 1133.

[27] Thomassinus, Pars II, lib. III, cap. 52, n. 5.

[28] Namely, the VI Council of Arles, the Council of Mainz, the II Council of Reims, the III Council of Tours, the II Council of Chalon-sur-Saône; cf. *MGH, Conc.*, II, pars II, 248-293.

[29] Cf. Hinschius, II, 7.

yet this factor obviously accelerated a decline in the celebration of provincial councils, since the metropolitan could no longer effectively command the presence of his suffragan bishops.[30] Another possible source of trouble in the celebration of councils derived from the factor of interference on the part of the civil authority.[31]

3. From the IV Council of the Lateran to the Council of Trent

The tendency to a relaxation of conciliar discipline was to continue, despite the decree of the IV Council of the Lateran in the year 1215. This Ecumenical Council in its sixth canon enacted that a provincial council should be held each year.[32] In his commentary on this canon, Hostiensis (Henricus de Segusio, +1271) stated that at best it had become the general practice to hold provincial councils every other year.[33] In Spain, the Council of Valladolid (1322) was constrained to decree that a metropolitan who culpably neglected to call a council at least within the two year period would automatically incur a personal interdict.[34] In 1364, Pope Urban V (1362-1370) in writing to all archbishops urged the celebration of provincial councils, and he requested a report from them on the pro-

[30] Cf. *infra*, pp. 15, 16.

[31] Can. 6, II Council of Nicaea (787): ". . . si quisquam princeps inventus fuerit hoc prohibere, communione privetur."—c. 7, D. XVIII; can. 32, Council of Meaux-Paris (845-846)—Mansi, XIV, 826; can. 17, IV Council of Constantinople (869-870)—Mansi, XVI, 171.

[32] Mansi, XXII, 991; c. 25, X, *de accusationibus, inquisitionibus et denunciationibus*, V, 1.

[33] *Commentaria in Quinque Decretalium Libros* (5 vols. in 3, Venetiis, 1581), Lib. V, tit. 1, *de accusationibus, inquisitionibus et denunciationibus*, cap. 25, n. 1: "Hoc [the rule of yearly councils] tamen pauci Metropolitani servant, quia aliqui nunquam istud concilium celebrant. Alii vix semel in vita sua, et qui melius faciunt, consueverunt hoc de biennio in biennium celebrare. . ." (Hereafter cited as Hostiensis.)

[34] Can. 1—Mansi, XXV, 697. For earlier penal legislation against the neglect of celebrating councils, cf. *infra*, pp. 11-14.

ceedings of the councils.[35] A letter of Pope Gregory XI (1370-1378), written in 1373 to the Archbishop of Narbonne, spoke of the neglect in the celebration of provincial councils almost everywhere.[36]

Finally, at the Council of Constance (1414-1418) came a statute calling for provincial councils only every third year. This statute was approved by Pope Martin V (1419-1431) in the year 1425.[37] The reason for the change in legislation may be discerned from the remark of a contemporary canonist, Panormitanus (Nicolaus de Tudeschis +1453), who commented sadly on the non-celebration of councils.[38] The new law prescribing a provincial council's celebration every three years was inserted by Pope Leo X in his Constitution "*Regimini universalis*" on May 4, 1515,[39] at the V Council of the Lateran.[40] The same law regarding the frequent celebration of councils was treated again at the Council of Trent.

This insistent legislation seems to leave no room for doubt that the law of celebrating the provincial council was, from the beginning, of serious proportions in the mind of the Church. But the question of the practical enforcement of the law was almost always a complex and vexing one.

[35] ". . . Nobis de convocatione huiusmodi, cum eam feceris, et demum de gestis in eodem concilio rescripturus."—Baronius, *Annales Ecclesiastici,* XXVI, p. 100, n. 23.

[36] ". . . celebratio huiusmodi fere ubique terrarum, quod dolentur referimus, longis temporibus est negligenter omissa."—Mansi, XXVI, 591.

[37] Wernz, II, n. 853.

[38] Secundo notatur quod ista, concilium provinciale et episcopale, debent necessario fieri singulis annis, et olim fiebant bis in anno, de quo in c. *quoniam,* 18 dist., sed hodie, et male, communiter non celebrantur."—*Commentaria in Quinque Decretalium Libros,* Lib. V, tit. 1, *de accusationibus, inquisitionibus et denunciationibus,* cap. 25, n. 1.

[39] N. 12—*Codicis Iuris Canonici Fontes,* cura Emi Petri Card. Gasparri editi (9 vols., Romae: Typis Polyglottis Vaticanis, 1923-1939 [Vols. VII-IX, ed. cura et studio Emi Iustiniani Card. Serédi]), n. 66. (Hereafter cited as *Fontes.*)

[40] Sess. X.

B. Remedies Employed Against Conciliar Decline

1. Specification of Excusing Causes

a. From the Celebration

Among the common law decrees concerning causes excusing from the celebration of councils, ill health, other urgent necessities and unavoidable matters of business were mentioned by the Council of Chalcedon (451).[41] Necessity, force and any reasonable obstacle were enumerated as valid excuses by the II Council of Nicaea (787).[42]

b. From Attendance

"Sufficiently grave necessity" was the excuse admitted by the IV Council Carthage (398), with the additional proviso that the impeded bishop must send a proxy to take his place at the council.[43] The further restriction came from the V Council of Carthage (401) that the absent bishop must explain the cause of his absence through a letter.[44]

Other legitimate excuses included a royal command,[45] old age,[46] death or illness of relatives, persecution, shipwreck, storms, floods,[47] interference by civil authority [48] and warfare.[49]

[41] C. 6, D. XVIII; can. 19, Council of Chalcedon (451)—Bruns, I, 30; cf. Mansi, VII, 389, 390.

[42] C. 7, D. XVIII; can. 6, II Council of Nicaea (787)—Mansi, XIII, 425-428.

[43] Can. 2—Bruns, I, 43; c. 9, D. XVIII.

[44] C. 10, D. XVIII. The commentators upon the *Decretum Gratiani* (ca. 1140) stated that this excuse could be delivered through a messenger; cf. *Glossa ordinaria,* c. 10, D. XVIII, ad v. *litteratorie.*

[45] Can. 35, Council of Agde (506): ". . . praeceptione regia. . ."—Bruns, II, 153; c. 13, D. XVIII.

[46] C. 10, D. XVIII.

[47] *Glossa ordinaria,* c. 6, D. XVIII, ad v. *necessitatibus.*

[48] Can. 15, XI Council of Toledo (675)—Bruns, I, 316.

[49] Can. 1, III Council of Orleans (538)—Bruns, II, 191; can. 17, IV Council of Constantinople (869-870)—Mansi, XVI, 171.

2. Sanctions

Penalties for negligence in convoking or attending the provincial council appear, at first sight, to be severe, for they included excommunication [50] and suspension from office.[51] But closer examination will reveal the very restricted sense of these sanctions.

a. Earlier Penalties—Excommunication

The penalty of excommunication was invoked in canon 10 of the V Council of Carthage (401),[52] in canon 19 of the Council of Arles (443 or 452),[53] in canon 35 of the Council of Agde (506) [54] and in canon 6 of the Council of Tarragona (516).[55] A year's excommunication was the sanction imposed by the XI Council of Toledo (675) for an unlawful absence from the council.[56] But, according to Fagnanus (1598-1678), even this penalty of the XI Council of Toledo, which was explicitly termed an excommunication, did not mean excommunication as it was later understood.[57]

What all of these episcopal excommunications really involved becomes clearer from the expression of the V Council of Carthage (401): ". . . *ecclesiae suae communione debent esse contenti.*" [58] This penalty was an exclusion, not from the sacraments and divine offices, but merely from the functions of the bishops in common, such

[50] Cc. 5, 12, 13, 14, D. XVIII.

[51] C. 25, X, *de accusationibus, inquisitionibus et denunciationibus,* V, 1.

[52] C. 10, D. XVIII.

[53] ". . . alienatum se a fratrum communione agnoscat: nec eum recipi liceat, nisi in sequenti synodo fuerit absolutus."—Bruns, II, 133; c. 12, D. XVIII.

[54] Bruns, II, 153. (There are very minor textual changes in this canon as it appears in c. 13, D. XVIII.)

[55] ". . . usque ad futurum concilium cunctorum episcoporum caritatis communione privetur."—Bruns, II, 16; c. 14, D. XVIII.

[56] Can. 15: ". . . Quisquis autem episcoporum excepta inevitabili causa vel necessitate de peragendo se concilio absentaverit, unius anni excommunicatione plectendus est. . ."—Bruns, I, 316.

[57] *Commentaria in Quinque Decretalium Libros* (5 vols. in 4, Venetiis, 1709), Lib. V, tit. 1, cap. 25, n. 111 (hereafter cited as Fagnanus). Note also that it is a penalty for a determinate time, unlike excommunication today, which is always a censure; cf. canon 2255, § 2, of the present Code.

[58] C. 10, D. XVIII.

as the consecrations of bishops, or the joint deliberations of bishops.[59] Apart from these official gatherings, social intercourse with the other bishops was not forbidden.[60] All of the sanctions of excommunication as considered above apparently had this restrictive sense,[61] and the differences of phraseology expressed the same substantial penalty,[62] namely, a bishop's exclusion from the community of bishops, without the surrender of his rights or office within his own proper diocese.[63] The deferring of absolution to the time of the next council[64] was considered to increase the shame of the penalty, and was done also in cases of sacrilege.[65]

b. Suspension

The penalty of excommunication, as described above, arose from the legislation of particular councils. The first Ecumenical Council to enact a penalty for the neglect of celebrating provincial councils

[59] *Glossa ordinaria,* c. 10, D. XVIII, ad v. *communione*; Rufinus, *Summa Decretorum,* ad c. 10, D. XVIII: ". . . tantum ecclesiae suae communicabunt." Rufinus mentioned that in c. un., C. 4, q. 5, the excommunication of the bishop for failing to appear when *accused* of a crime was an excommunication from the community of all Christians, but here the case was different.

[60] Fagnanus, Lib. V, tit. 1, cap. 25, n. 111.

[61] Fagnanus, *loc. cit.*; cf. *Glossa ordinaria,* c. 3, C. V, q. 4, ad v. *excommunicationis*: ". . . a consortio fratrum."

[62] E.g., c. 13, D. XVIII: ". . . a caritate fratrum et ecclesiae communione priventur" and c. 12, D. XVIII: ". . . alienatum . . . a fratrum communione. . ."

[63] The penalty which was invoked by the Council of Laodicaea (343-380), in canon 40, was interpreted by the twelfth century Glossators as referring to this type of excommunication; cf. *Glossa ordinaria,* c. 5, D. XVIII, ad v. *accusare*: "debent excommunicari." The original penalty, however, appears to have been more indefinite; cf. canon 40: ". . . εἰ δὲ καταφρονήσειεν, ὁ τοιοῦτος ἑαυτὸν αἰτιάσεται. . ."—Bruns, I, 78; c. 5, D. XVIII: ". . . quod si contempserint, se ipsos videntur accusare. . ." A very similar penalty, enacted in canon 19 of the II Council of Braga (572), which was evidently patterned upon that of Laodicaea, was framed: ". . . reus erit fraterni concilii."—Bruns, II, 48.

[64] C. 13, D. XVIII: ". . . usque ad proximam synodum. . ."; c. 14, D. XVIII: ". . . usque ad futurum concilium. . ."; c. 12, D. XVIII.

[65] *Glossa ordinaria,* c. 12, D. XVIII, ad v. *nisi in sequenti synodo.*

was that of Chalcedon (451), whose nineteenth canon mildly stated that a neglectful bishop could be lawfully corrected by means of a fraternal admonition.[66]

The II Council of Nicaea (787), in canon 6, made a negligent metropolitan "subject to canonical penalties"—a rather vague sanction, unless it became applicable through more concrete penalties of the particular law in a given locality.[67]

Suspension from office and benefice was the sanction invoked in 1215 by the IV Council of the Lateran.[68] This penalty was restated in a modified form in the Decretals of Pope Gregory IX in 1234—consisting now in suspension from office alone:

> Quisquis autem hoc salutare statutum neglexerit adimplere a sui executione officii suspendatur [donec per superioris arbitrium eius relaxatur].[69]

It was applicable to negligent metropolitans and negligent suffragan bishops alike.[70] But this was only a *ferendae sententiae* penalty, according to Hostiensis (+ 1271)[71] and Ioannes Andreae (+ 1348).[72] This suspension from office remained a *ferendae sententiae* penalty through the following centuries, and was so interpreted by Pope Leo X in 1515.[73] Consequently, the sanction had

[66] C. 6, D. XVIII: ". . . licere eos fraternae caritatis admonitionibus corripi."

[67] C. 7, D. XVIII.

[68] Can. 6: ". . .a suis beneficiis et executione officii suspendatur. . ."—Mansi, XXII, 991.

[69] C. 25, X, *de accusationibus, inquisitionibus et denunciationibus,* V, 1.

[70] Hostiensis, Lib. V, tit. 1, cap. 25, n. 9.

[71] *Loc. cit.*: "Non est ergo poena latae sententiae, sed ferendae, quod bene expedit, nam et si omnes negligentes suspenderentur, pauci possent exequi, quod incumbit."

[72] *In Quinque Decretarium Libros Novella Commentaria* (5 vols. in 4, Venetiis, 1581), Lib. V, tit. 1, cap. 25, n. 8, ad v. *suspendatur*: ". . . est ergo canon ferendae sententiae."

[73] Const. *"Regimini universalis,"* 4 maii, 1515, n. 12: "Circa hoc autem negligentes poenas in eisdem canonibus contentas se noverint *incursuros*."—*Fontes*, n. 66. Cf. Fagnanus, lib. V, tit. 1, cap. 25, n. 107, concerning this use of *incursuros* as designating a *ferendae sententiae* penalty.

little practical effect, for it remained a threat of punishment which was not carried into execution.[74]

c. Other Penalties

A striking example of the enactment of a *latae sententiae* censure (personal interdict) against negligent metropolitans appeared in 1322 at the Council of Valladolid.[75] Examples of other sanctions invoked by provincial councils are: a year's suspension from celebrating Mass (against metropolitans),[76] suspension from office *"donec satisfaciat fratribus"* (against suffragan bishops),[77] personal accountability to the archbishop (against suffragans),[78] and money fines (against suffragan bishops).[79]

In order to insure the successful completion of conciliar business, there were sanctions against: leaving the council before its conclusion (punished with excommunication),[80] provoking disorder at the council (punished with excommunication of three days),[81] a metropolitan's exacting of gifts from his suffragans (punished with fourfold restitution),[82] a secular prince's interfering with the work of the council (punished with excommunication),[83] and the illegitimate absenting of themselves from a council on the part of abbots and conventual priors (punished with a personal interdict of a month, with severer penalties for the *recidivi*).[84]

[74] Hostiensis, Lib. V, tit. 1, cap. 25, n. 9; Thomassinus, Pars II, lib. III, cap. 57, n. 5.

[75] Can. 1. ". . . si archiepiscopi, saltem in biennio semel loco et tempore opportunis, per se vel per alios, quatenus de iure conceditur, ipsis legitimis impeditis, celebrare concilia omiserint, eo ipso tamdiu ab ingressu ecclesiae sint suspensi, donec negligentiam suam purgaverint provincia concilia celebrando."—Mansi, XXV, 697.

[76] Can. 1, III Council of Orleans (538)—Bruns, II, 191, 192; Mansi, IX, 11.

[77] Can. 33, Council of Meaux-Paris (845-846)—Mansi, XIV, 826.

[78] Can. 15, Council of Tarragona (1329)—Mansi, XXV, 842.

[79] Can. 70, Council of Benevento (1331)—Mansi, XXV, 973; can. 70, Council of Benevento (1378)—Mansi, XXVI, 654.

[80] Can. 19, Council of Arles (443 or 452)—Bruns, II, 133; c. 12, D. XVIII.

[81] Can. 1, XI Council of Toledo (675)—Bruns, I, 308; c. 3, C. V, q. 4.

[82] Can. 6, II Council of Nicaea (787)—c. 7, D. XVIII.

[83] C. 7, D. XVIII.

[84] Can. 1, Council of Paris (1248)—Mansi, XXIII, 765.

3. Specification of the Exact Day for the Council

A very practical measure, which favored regularity in the celebrating of councils, was the policy, as adopted by certain provincial councils, of determining at each conciliar meeting the day of the next council. In 441 the I Council of Orange ordained that each provincial council was to prescribe the time and the place for the celebration of the next council.[85] Similarly, the decrees of the IV Council of Toledo (633)[86] and of the Council of Benevento (1331)[87] specified the exact day for the celebration of the subsequent council.

Article 2. Operation of the Provincial Council

A. Modal Factors

Most of the features connected with the operation of the provincial council remained essentially unchanged through the centuries. This accounts for the relative dearth of legislation, in the *Corpus Iuris Canonici,* concerning the provincial council, which reached its complete formation at an early stage in the Church's history.

1. Convocation

Around the metropolitan pivoted the functioning and, it may be added, the fortunes of the provincial council. Even after the metropolitan lost his jurisdictional authority over the suffragan bishops, he retained the key position in the holding of councils.

To the metropolitan belonged the rights of convoking and of presiding at the council.[88] These powers were not to be exercised by

[85] Can. 29—Bruns, II, 126.

[86] Can. 3—Bruns, I, 222.

[87] Can. 70—Mansi, XXV, 973.

[88] Can. 18, II Council of Braga (572): ". . . vocante metropolitano episcopo omnes provinciae episcopos. . ."—Bruns, II, 47.

Can. 6, IV Council of the Lateran (1215): "Sicut olim a sanctis Patribus noscitur institutum, metropolitani singulis annis . . . provincialia non omittant concilia celebrare. . ."—Mansi, XXII, 991; c. 25, X, *de accusationibus, inqui-*

any other bishop in the province.[89] Moreover, the convocation of the provincial council by the metropolitan was not only his right, but his official obligation, binding under canonical sanctions.[90]

It was the office of the metropolitan to notify the suffragan bishops, calling them to the council.[91] One such citation or call to a council by the metropolitan sufficed to make a negligent suffragan bishop subject to penalties.[92] The metropolitan, according to the spirit of the law, was to consult the interests of the suffragan bishops by selecting a place not too remote.[93] But the III Council of Orleans (538) declared that ill health or any other grave necessity on his part would justify the metropolitan in transferring the council from an already appointed place to the metropolitan city.[94]

To give added encouragement and prestige to councils and to offset every unwanted decline, the Holy See manifested its interest in a special way. From the eleventh century onward provincial councils were sometimes convoked by Legates, sent by the Holy Father to help expedite the celebration of these councils.[95]

2. Attendance and Precedence

The metropolitan presided and kept order at the council.[96]

sitionibus et denunciationibus, V, 1; can. 16, Council of Antioch (341)—Bruns, I, 85; can. 17, IV Council of Constantinople (869-870)—Mansi, XVI, 171; Fagnanus, Lib. V, tit. 1, cap. 25, n. 99.

[89] C. 4, D. XVIII.

[90] Cc. 4, 6, 13, D. XVIII; can. 1, III Council of Orleans (538)—Bruns, II, 191, 192; cf. also *supra,* Article 1, B, 2, *Sanctions,* pp. 11-14.

[91] Can. 35, Council of Agde (506): "Si episcopus metropolitanus ad comprovinciales episcopus epistolas direxerit in quibus eos . . . ad synodum invitet. . ."—Bruns, II, 153; cc. 4, 13, D. XVIII; can. 1, III Council of Orleans (538)—Bruns, II, 191, 192.

[92] *Glossa ordinaria,* c. 13, D. XVIII, ad v. *praeceptione regia.*

[93] C. 7, D. XXVIII; Fagnanus, Lib. V, tit. 1, cap. 25, n. 18; can. 20, II Council of Mâcon (585)—Bruns, II, 255.

[94] Can. 1—Bruns, II, 191, 192; Mansi, IX, 11.

[95] Wernz, II, n. 853, note 106.

[96] Can. 16, Council of Antioch (341): "τελείαν δὲ ἐκείνην εἶναι σύνοδον ᾗ συμπάρεστι καὶ ὁ τῆς μητροπόλεως."—Bruns, I, 85; cc. 1, 4, 15, D. XVIII: Fagnanus, Lib. V, tit. 1, cap. 25, n. 99.

clearly, in the year 448, at the Council of Constantinople, where archimandrites (monastic superiors) signed the *acta* of the council, but only with the single word, "ὑπέγραψα" (i. e., "*subscripsi*").[110] The Council of Langres (830) serves as another example. Among the signatures at this Council are those of two chorepiscopi, of two abbots, and of priests and deacons, and their manner of signing the decrees observes the distinction noted above. They were permitted to sign their names, but were not permitted to give a definitive vote.[111]

With the possible exception, then, of procurators, only the metropolitan and the provincial bishops had a decisive vote.[112]

Each suffragan bishop was required to publish the provincial conciliar decrees through the medium of a diocesan synod, which, by a ruling of the XVI Council of Toledo (693), was to be held within six months of the conclusion of the provincial council.[113] The IV Council of the Lateran (1215) prescribed that diocesan synods be held yearly for this purpose.[114]

B. Sphere of Legislation

In the early Church there were frequent and pressing demands for conciliar activity. A universal corpus of law had not been formulated, and the process of forming this law was largely entrusted to councils, even until the appearance of Gratian's *Decretum* in the twelfth century.[115]

110 Mansi, VI, 747-754. Other early examples of such subscriptions are found in Councils of Rome in the early sixth century; cf. Thiel, *Epistolae Romanorum Pontificum Genuinae et Quae ad Eos Scriptae Sunt a S. Hilario usque ad Pelagium II*, Vol. I (Brunsbergae, 1868), p. 682, note 6, and *ibid.*, pp. 648-654, 692-695; cf. also Mansi, VIII, 268, 269, 299-302, 307, 308.

111 Mansi, XIV, 629, 630.

112 Cc. 4, 14, D. XVIII; Wernz, II, n. 853.

113 Can. 7—Bruns, I, 372; c. 17, D. XVIII.

114 Can. 6—Mansi, XXII, 991; c. 25, X, *de accusationibus, inquisitionibus et denunciationibus*, V, 1.

115 E. g., from the Council of Elvira (ca. 305) the following canons were later received into the *Corpus Iuris Canonici*: can. 52 (*apud* Bruns, I, 8), as c. 3, C. V, q. 1; can. 54 (*apud* Bruns, I, 9), as c. 1, C. XXXI, q. 3; can. 72 (*apud* Bruns, I, 11) as c. 7, C. XXXI, q. 1; can. 73 (*apud* Bruns, I, 11), as c. 6, C. V, q. 6.

Matters treated by the ancient councils, according to the discipline then prevailing, embraced a wide field, extending even to questions concerning the election of bishops.[116] With the progress of the years and the formation of a body of laws the field of new conciliar legislation naturally became narrowed. But, in every century particular problems which arose in a particular place had to be met with particular legislation. In the province this was the office of the provincial council.[117]

Obviously the provincial councils contained only particular jurisdiction. Their laws were binding upon the whole territory of the particular province.[118]

What developed into the chief sphere of provincial legislation was the office of correction. Upon the provincial council, through the centuries, devolved the responsibility of correcting aberrations from the law by means of specific provisions adapted to the time and place of a given locality. As the necessity of making new laws grew less with the formation of a stable *Corpus Iuris,* the office of corrective legislation became more and more important. To preserve good ecclesiastical order throughout a province, to give unity and strength to the observance of ecclesiastical discipline, there were repeated demands for correcting deviations as they crept in, which was often stressed as the end of provincial legislation.[119]

[116] Can. 4, I Council of Nicaea (325)—Mansi, II, 669; can. 19, Council of Antioch (341)—Bruns, I, 85; Mansi, II, 1316; Wernz-Vidal, *Ius Canonicum* (7 vols in 8, Romae: Apud Aedes Universitatis Gregorianae, 1925-1938; Vol. II, 3. ed., 1943), II, 671, 672 (hereafter cited as Wernz-Vidal).

[117] Can. 20, Council of Antioch (341)—Bruns, I, 85; Bouix, *De Concilio Provinciali,* p. 22.

[118] Can. 2, I Ecumenical Council of Constantinople (381)—Mansi, III, 560.

[119] C. 6, D. XVIII: "Pervenit ad nostras aures quod in provinciis constituta episcoporum concilia minime celebrentur. Hoc ex eo probatur, quod multae, quae correctione opus habent, ecclesiasticae res negligantur." (From can. 19, Council of Chalcedon [451].)

Can. 1, I Council of Auvergne (535): ". . . ea quae ad emendationem vitae, ad severitatem regulae, ad animae remedia pertinent."—Bruns, II, 188. (The reference here, as in the citations to follow below, is to the proper object of provincial legislation.)

For example, the renowned Council of Elvira (ca. 305) treated questions concerning idolatry, dangers to morality, sanctions to safeguard morals, disciplinary rules for the clergy, celibacy, emergency baptism, repentant apostates.[120] The Council of Gerona (517) issued decrees concerning the Mass, litanies, day for baptism, emergency baptism, rules of conduct for clerics, public penitents, and the divine office.[121]

Finally, it was not enough to have a practical body of laws. That law had to be well known and had to be universally applied to become effective. The publication of the law and the practical insistence upon it in a given province was made the jurisdictional responsibility of the provincial council, a function which became of the greater importance when the metropolitan was relieved, almost entirely, of any kindred responsibility in the matter.[122]

Can. 18, II Council of Braga (572): "Propter ecclesiasticas curas . . ."—Bruns, II, 47; cf. c. 15, D. XVIII: "Propter ecclesiasticas causas . . ."

Can. 20, II Council of Mâcon (585): ". . . causas exsurgentes tam divinae religionis quam humanae necessitatis discutiant . . ."—Bruns, II, 255.

C. 7, D. XVIII: ". . . depravata corrigi." (From can. 6, II Council of Nicaea [787].)

Can. 6, IV Council of the Lateran (1215): "Sicut olim a sanctis Patribus noscitur institutum, metropolitani singulis annis cum suis suffraganeis provincialia non omittant concilia celebrare, in quibus de corrigendis excessibus et moribus reformandis, praesertim in clero, diligentem habeant cum Dei timore tractatum, canonicas regulas, et maxime, quae statutae sunt in hoc generali concilio, relegentes . . ."—Mansi, XXII, 991.

Leo X (in Conc. Lateranen. V), const. "*Regimini universalis,*" 4 maii 1515, n. 12: ". . . pro morum correctione et contraversiarum decisione et determinatione ac mandatorum Domini observatione, fieri debere concilium provinciale ac synodum episcopalem, ut depravata corrigerentur . . ."—*Fontes*, n. 66.

Glossa ordinaria, casus to D. XVIII: ". . . ad correctionem . . ."

[120] Bruns, I, 2-12; Mansi, II, 5-19.

[121] Bruns, II, 18-20; cf. also the preceding pages of this Chapter for examples of provincial laws.

[122] Can. 6, IV Council of the Lateran (1215): ". . . et maxime, quae statuta sunt in hoc generali concilio, relegentes, ut eas faciant observari, debitam poenam transgressoribus infligendo."—Mansi, XXII, 991; c. 25, X, *de accusationibus, inquisitionibus, et denunciationibus*, V, 1.

CHAPTER II

LEGISLATION FROM THE COUNCIL OF TRENT TO THE PRESENT CODE

Article 1. New Legislation by the Council of Trent

Canonical legislation concerning the provincial councils was further particularized by the Council of Trent (1545-1563). It was enacted that, if the metropolitan was legitimately impeded from convoking a council, this obligation devolved upon the senior suffragan bishop.[1] Within a year after the conclusion of the Council of Trent, and thereafter at least every three years, provincial councils were to be called in accordance with the already existing law.[2]

Conciliar discipline was also strengthened by the requirement that "exempt" bishops (i.e., those who were not under the jurisdiction of any metropolitan, and were therefore, strictly considered, outside the jurisdictional limits of any province) became obliged to select a neighboring metropolitan bishop, and thenceforth to participate in his provincial councils, and to effect the observance in their own diocese of the conciliar decrees.[3]

[1] Sess. XXIV, *de ref.*, c. 2; cf. canon 284, 2°, of the present Code, similarly.

[2] "Provincialia Concilia, sicubi omissa sunt, pro moderandis moribus, corrigendis excessibus, controversiis componendis, aliisque ex sacris canonibus permissis renoventur. Quare metropolitani per se ipsos, seu, illis legitime impeditis, coepiscopus antiquior intra annum ad minus a fine praesentis Concilii, et deinde quolibet saltem triennio post octavam Paschae Resurrectionis Domini nostri Iesu Christi, seu alio commodiori tempore, pro more provinciae, non praetermittat Synodum in provincia sua cogere: quo episcopi omnes, et alii, qui de iure, vel consuetudine interesse debent, exceptis iis, quibus cum imminenti periculo transfretandum esset, convenire omnino teneantur."—Sess. XXIV, *de ref.*, c. 2.

[3] *Loc. cit.*: "Itidem episcopi, qui nulli archiepiscopo subiiciuntur, aliquem vicinum metropolitanum semel eligant, in cuius Synodo provinciali cum aliis interesse debeant; et quae ibi ordinata fuerint, observent, ac observari faciant. In reliquis omnibus eorum exemptio et privilegia salva atque integra maneant."

A particular object recommended to the legislative competency of the provincial councils was the regulating of details concerning the examination of candidates for the pastoral office; cf. sess. XXIV, *de ref.*, c. 18; cf. also Fagnanus, Lib. V, tit. 1, cap. 25, n. 51.

Article 2. Frequency of Celebrating the Provincial Council

The Council of Trent, as just noted, reiterated the law calling for the celebration of provincial councils at least every three years.[4] The prevailing *ferendae sententiae* sanction of suspension from office levelled against negligent metropolitans and suffragan bishops was also kept in force.[5]

There is little need of multiplying details to prove the non-observance of this law. Within a century after the Council of Trent, except in the Province of Tarragona, councils were neglected nearly everywhere.[6] With few exceptions this condition was to grow even worse until the nineteenth century.[7]

In some cases the blame rested upon metropolitans, but often there were compelling circumstances which made it appear more prudent not tò call a council at all. The chief difficulty lay in turbulent political conditions and in the encroachment of the King upon the domain of things spiritual.[8] The shadow of Gallicanism appeared over the Church in the sixteenth century,[9] and spread from France to other countries.[10] The "most Christian" King did not allow

[4] Sess. XXIV, *de ref.*, c. 2.

[5] *Loc. cit.*, "Quod si in his tam metropolitani, quam episcopi, et alii suprascripti negligentes fuerint, poenas, sacris canonibus sancitas, incurrant." Cf. c. 25, X, *de accusationibus, inquisitionibus et denunciationibus*, V, 1.

[6] *Acta et Decreta Sacrorum Conciliorum Recentiorum, Collectio Lacensis* (7 vols., auctoribus G. Schneemann [Vols. I-VI] et T. Granderath [Vol. VII], Friburgi Brisgoviae, 1870-1890) I, 1, a (hereafter cited as *Coll. Lac.*). In 1579 three exempt bishops who had failed to comply with the Tridentine law were ordered to select the Province of Cosenza as their own, and to attend the provincial council there on the Pentecost following. Cf. S. C. C., *Cusentina*, 20 ian. 1579—*Fontes*, n. 1350; *Cassanen*, 20 ian. 1579—*Fontes*, n. 1349.

[7] Council of Rome (1725), tit. II, c. 2: ". . . Episcoporum Concilia minime vel raro sunt celebrata . . ."—*Coll. Lac.*, I, 351, a, b; 4, a; 19, a; André, *Cours Alphabétique et Méthodique de Droit Canon* (2 vols. in 4, Paris, 1844), I, tom. I, 575. In some places a full century elapsed between provincial councils: cf. S. C. C., *Senen.*, 28 nov. 1699—*Fontes*, n. 2973; Bouix, pp. 45-53; De Hericourt, *Les Loix Ecclésiastiques de France* (nouvelle ed., Paris, 1771), p. 277.

[8] *Coll. Lac.*, I, 19, a.

[9] Wernz, II, n. 854.

[10] *Coll. Lac.*, I, 18, c, d.

councils to be celebrated without his permission, and he steadfastly refused that permission.[11] In retrospect, however, it has been said that God's Providence restricted councils almost to non-existence in an age when their celebration could have been perilous precisely because of the dangers of intrusion by the King.[12]

The course of the nineteenth century proved a happier era in the restoration of conciliar discipline.[13] In the United States, the seven Provincial Councils of Baltimore were celebrated between the years 1829 and 1849.[14] In 1848, and after, conferences of bishops were held at times as a sort of substitute for provincial councils, and were the historical forerunner of the conferences preliminary to councils, as prescribed in canon 292 of the present Code.[15]

The Tridentine law of holding councils every three years was reaffirmed in 1725 by Pope Benedict XIII (1724-1730) at the Council of Rome.[16] The Fathers of the Vatican Council (1869-1870) considered modifying the law relative to the celebration of provincial councils by specifying a period of five years, but this proposal was not passed.[17] The present law of the Code calls for the celebration of a provincial council at least once in each period of twenty years.[18]

Article 3. The Constitution *"Immensa Aeterni"*

During the twenty-odd years following the Council of Trent, provincial councils spontaneously adopted the practice of submitting their decrees, before promulgation, to the approval of the Holy See.[19]

[11] Bouix, pp. 45-53; *Coll. Lac.*, I, 5, c. As an example of the royal domination over spiritual matters, in 1811 Napoleon convoked a so-called "National Council."—*Coll. Lac.*, IV, 1223-1320.

[12] *Coll. Lac.*, I, 19, a.

[13] *Coll. Lac.*, I, 18, a; 20; Wernz-Vidal, II, 673.

[14] Cf. Guilday, *A History of the Councils of Baltimore* (New York: Macmillan, 1932), pp. 81-163.

[15] Coronata, *Institutiones Iuris Canonici* (5 vols., Taurini: Marietti, 1928-1936), I, 428. (Hereafter cited as *Inst.*)

[16] *Coll. Lac.*, I, 4, b; 351, a, b.

[17] Wernz-Vidal, II, 673, 674.

[18] Canon 283.

[19] Cf. *Coll. Lac.*, I, 16, d; 17, a, b, for examples.

This was a measure of prudence, a safeguard against conflicts with the common law, and against ambiguities in the conciliar expression regarding dogma or discipline. It also added the approbation of the highest ecclesiastical authority, thereby assuring greater prestige and security to provincial legislation.[20] Pope Sixtus V (1585-1590), in his Constitution *"Immensa aeterni,"* on January 22, 1588, enacted as part of the universal law that before being promulgated all the *acta* of provincial councils should be submitted to the Sacred Congregation of the Council for examination and revision.[21] One may here quote from the Pastoral Letter of the II Plenary Council of Baltimore (1866):

> By a wise regulation . . . which combines the benefit of central authority with the advantages of local legislation, the decrees of such Councils are not promulgated or published, until they have been submitted to the Holy See. This is not only for the purpose of imparting to them a still higher authority, but also to guard against any inaccuracy in doctrinal statements, or any enactment not in conformity with the general discipline of the Church, or that might be contrary to the spirit of Ecclesiastical legislation.[22]

[20] *Coll. Lac.*, I, 17, d; 18, b. This approbation of the Holy See is not to be considered a positive confirmation, nor does it intrinsically change the nature of the conciliar *acta* and decrees. Cf. *infra*, pp. 49, 50.

[21] "Et quoniam eodem concilio Tridentino decretum est synodos provinciales tertio quoque anno . . . id in executionis usum ab iis, quorum interest, induci eadem congregatio providebit. Provincialium vero, ubivis terrarum illae celebrentur, decreta ad se [S. C. C.] mitti praecipiet, eaque singula expendet et recognoscet."—*Bullarum Diplomatum et Privilegiorum Sanctorum Romanorum Pontificum Taurinensis Editio* (24 vols. in 25, 1857-1883, Vol. VIII, Neapoli, 1883), VIII, 991. (Hereafter cited as *Bull. Rom. Taur.*) Cf. Wernz, I, n. 181, note 42: "Antequam recognitionem illam factam acta et decreta Concil. partic. promulgari valide non possunt. Cf. S. C. C., 6 apr. 1596." This declaration of the S. C. C. (not contained in the *Fontes* or the *Collect.*) is quoted by Petra (*Commentaria ad Constitutiones Apostolicas* [5 vols. in 2, Venetiis, 1729], I, p. 284, n. 121): "Decreta, quae in Conciliis Provincialibus conduntur, publicari non debent inconsulto Romano Pontifice." (Petra's work hereafter will be cited as *Commentaria.*) Cf. Bouix, p. 371; cf. *infra*, pp. 48-52.

[22] *Coll. Lac.*, III, 1249, b.

The Constitution of Sixtus V remained the final legislation on the constitutive law of the provincial council until the time of the present Code.[23]

Article 4. Other Pronouncements of the Holy See

A. Convocation

As previously noted, the senior suffragan bishop of the province was under obligation of convoking the council when the metropolitan was legitimately impeded from doing so.[24] This included periods in which the metropolitan see was vacant.[25] An exempt bishop could not convoke the council.[26]

B. Due Order and Voting

The metropolitan presided and kept order at the council, but he could not, without the consent of the other bishops, adjourn the council, nor could he definitively order some measure to be introduced or put aside.[27]

[23] Wernz-Vidal, II, 673.

[24] Conc. Trident., sess. XXIV, *de ref.*, c. 2.

[25] S. C. C., *Tarraconen.*, 2 dec. 1623: "Sacra, etc. partibus auditis censuit ius Provinciale Concilium indicendi ac celebrandi sede vacante non ad Capitulum Metropolitanum, sed ad antiquiorem Provinciae Episcopum pertinere"—*Fontes*, n. 2444; cf. also S. C. C., *Tarraconen.*, 10 febr. 1624—*Fontes*, n. 2448.

[26] S. C. C., *Burgen.*, 17 apr. 1649—Maupied, *Juris Canonici Universi Compendium* (accurante J. P. Migne, 2 vols., Pariis, 1861), I, 456 (hereafter cited as Maupied); Fagnanus, Lib. V, tit. 1, cap. 25, n. 18. (This response is reported by Maupied and Fagnanus, but is not contained in the *Fontes* or in the *Collectanea S. Congregationis de Propaganda Fide* [2 vols., Romae: Typographia Polyglotta de Propaganda Fide, 1907]. The latter collection will hereafter be cited as *Collect.*)

[27] S. C. C., *Civitatis Regalis in Indiis* (*Limana*), mense febr. 1586, ad 6, 7—*Fontes*, n. 2152.

At the sole invitation of the metropolitan, bearing his signature, the cathedral chapter had the right of attending the council; cf. S. C. de Prop. Fide (*Angliae*), 6 iul., 1894, ad 1—*Collect.*, n. 1418.

Exempt bishops always had a decisive vote,[28] but the procurator of a bishop [29] had a decisive vote only with the consent of the members of the council.[30]

Only through the unanimous consent of the residential bishops could a titular bishop exercise a deliberative vote.[31]

C. Place of the Provincial Council in the Legislation of the Church

Provincial councils had true legislative power, which was superior to that of any individual bishop or metropolitan who was a member of the council.[32] From the exercise of this power derived many and singular benefits. For provincial conciliar legislation was a check upon evil and a power for good.[33] It combined effectively the benefits of local legislation and of central authority in an eminently practical way.[34] And that unity which is the chief mark of the

[28] S. C. C., *Tranen.*, mense iun. 1589—*Fontes*, n. 2208.

[29] S. C. C., *Tarraconen.*, 4 dec. 1638: ". . . Procuratores sint habiles, Doctores, et discreti."—*Fontes*, n. 2596.

[30] S. C. C., *Rothomagen.*, 1581—Maupied, I, 457; Fagnanus, Lib. V, tit. 1, cap. 25, n. 31. (This response is not contained in the *Fontes* or in the *Collect.*). Cf. canons 287, § 2, and 282, § 1, where the Code legislates that solely one's coadjutor or auxiliary bishop retains a decisive vote as proxy at the council.

[31] S. C. C., *Aquen.*, 24 aug. 1850—*Fontes*, n. 4112. (Cf. canon 286, § 2, where a majority vote of the constitutive members of the council now suffices to confer a deliberative vote upon a titular bishop.) This response of the Sacred Congregation also indicated that titular bishops by their seniority in the episcopacy do not obtain precedence over suffragan bishops at provincial councils.

[32] S. C. S. Off., 10 sept. 1896, ad 1, 2—*Fontes*, n. 1184; cf. also canon 291, § 2.

[33] Pius IX, ep. encycl. *"Cum nuper,"* 20 ian. 1858, n. 4: "Denique, Venerabiles Fratres, ut sanctissimae nostrae religionis bono et commendatarum Vobis ovium saluti magis ac magis consulere valeatis, summopere optamus ut Provincialia Concilia ex Sacrorum Canonum praescripto concelebranda curetis. Etenim probe intelligitis, hoc sane pacto Vos, et collatis inter Vos consiliis, et rebus omnibus mature perpensis, posse facilius et consultius opportuna malis adhibere remedia, et vestrarum Dioecesium prosperitati providere, et Dioecesanas deinde cogere Synodos, quae ex Canonicis Sanctionibus a Vobis sunt habendae." —*Fontes*, n. 523.

[34] Pastoral Letter, II Plenary Council of Baltimore (1866)—*Coll. Lac.*, III, 1249, b.

divinely founded Church became most strikingly apparent to those outside the fold when there was uniformity even, so far as was possible, in matters of discipline, and this was a specific end of provincial legislation.[35]

Thus it is that, through the long centuries of her legislative history, even to the present day, the constant solicitude of the sacred canons of the Church and the highest praise of the Supreme Pontiffs have been accorded to the celebration of provincial councils.[36]

[35] S. C. de Prop. Fide, litt. encycl. (ad Epp. Indiar.), 28 aug., 1893—*Collect.*, II, n. 1848. In this encyclical letter the celebration of provincial councils was termed a most apt means for the propagation of Christianity, and it was decreed that provincial councils should be held in all the provinces of the East Indies by April, 1894.

[36] S. C. de Prop. Fide, litt. encycl. (ad Epp. Indiar.), 28 aug. 1893: "Heic vero supervacaneum foret multis verbis huiusmodi synodorum utilitatem extollere; quum propter magna quae ex iis rei christianae promanant bona, earumdem coactio a sacris canonibus fuerit iamdiu praescripta, iterumque a Tridentino Concilio praecepta, ac per saeculorum tractum ab omnibus fere Pontificibus, sanctaeque Ecclesiae Patribus summopere semper fuit commendata." —*Collect.*, II, n. 1848.

Part Two

Canonical Commentary

CHAPTER III

PRINCIPLES GOVERNING PROVINCIAL LEGISLATION

Article 1. Nature of the Provincial Council

A. What is a Provincial Council?

Of major importance for every lawmaker must be the consideration of the needs of time and place and people. Circumstances that are local are a prime factor in the framing of wise laws which are aptly proportioned to the end to be attained. Holy Mother Church shows her wisdom and foresight in this matter. She sanctions reasonably established custom as a potentially valid instrument of law.[1] She upholds the provincial council as a canonical institution which will consult in particular detail the needs of a locality, geographically small in comparison to the Church as a whole, and yet a vital unit in true ecclesiastical discipline—the province.

Actually, while a parish is the smallest, a province is the largest, of the territorial divisions of the Church. An ecclesiastical province comprises several dioceses which are united under the presidency of a metropolitan or an archbishop, who holds this dignitary preeminence as a result of the recognition of his see as the metropolitan see by the Holy Father.[2] The metropolitan, however, does not possess episcopal

[1] Canons 25-30.

[2] Blat, *Commentarium Textus Codicis Iuris Canonici* (5 vols. in 6, Vol. II, *De Personis*, Romae, 1919; Vol. V, *De Delictis et Poenis*, Romae, 1924), II, 247. (Hereafter cited as *Commentarium*.)

jurisdictional authority over any diocese but his own.[3] The dioceses associated with the metropolitan see, and known as suffragan sees, are each ruled by their own bishop. But if the province is to be a true ecclesiastical unit, if there is to be harmony of laws and discipline, jurisdiction must be exercised over the entire territory, so that the dioceses will be mutually helpful in attaining the end for which the Church exists.

To the introductory question, then, the answer may be given: the provincial council is the legitimate assembly of the local ordinaries of an ecclesiastical province, for the purpose of deliberating upon, and of providing for, the ecclesiastical needs of that province, with true jurisdictional acts.[4] The term "local ordinaries" in the definition is to be understood as defined in the present Code, with the exception that vicars general are not here included.[5]

B. Powers

The jurisdictional powers of the provincial council are derived from the law of the present Code and are attached to the office which the prelates, when united in the conciliar assembly, exercise in their own name.[6] They are, therefore, to be classified as ordinary powers[7] and include legislative, executive and judiciary powers over the whole

[3] Cf. canons 273; 274; 276. Canon 274 confers upon the metropolitan only strictly delimited and emergency powers. The reader may await with interest the forthcoming work, *The Rights and Obligations of Metropolitans* (The Catholic University of America Canon Law Studies), by the Rev. Alphonse Popek.

[4] Wernz-Vidal, II, 669, 670; cf. *ibid.*, pp. 523, 681; Beste, *Introductio in Codicem* (2. ed., Collegeville, Minn.: St. John's Abbey Press, 1944), p. 231; Chelodi, *Ius de Personis iuxta Codicem Iuris Canonici* (2. ed., ab E. Bertagnolli recognita et aucta Tridenti: Libr. Edit. Tridentum, 1927), p. 386. (Hereafter cited as *Ius de Personis.*)

[5] Canon 198, § 1: In iure nomine *Ordinarii* intelliguntur . . . pro suo quisque territorio Episcopus residentialis, Abbas vel Praelatus *nullius* . . ., Administrator, Vicarius et Praefectus Apostolicus, itemque ii qui praedictis deficientibus interim ex iuris praescripto aut ex probatis constitutionibus succedunt in regimine . . . Cf. *infra*, pp. 90-99.

[6] Canon 290.

[7] Canon 197, § 1; Wernz-Vidal, II, 681.

territory subject to the jurisdiction of the council.[8] Paramount among these powers today is the legislative function.[9]

Conciliar legislative power is not a mere sum of the powers of the individual bishops; it is a higher power conferred by the law. It exceeds the episcopal power, for an individual bishop cannot legislate for any territory but his own, while conciliar decrees have force in the whole province, even over the bishops who constitute the council. Such decrees, therefore, transcend all episcopal and diocesan laws [10] and, according to the norms of canons 14, 13, and 92, they bind all persons dwelling in the province, including religious, without prejudice, however, to the exemptions granted to religious by the common law.[11]

Michiels [12] supports the opinion that the laws of provincial councils, unless they include an express derogatory clause, do not derogate diocesan statutes. This opinion is derived from canon 22, which states that a general law in no way diminishes the force of particular

[8] Toso, *Ad Codicem Juris Canonici Commentaria Minora* (5 vols. in 2, Vol. I, 2. ed. revisa, Torino-Romae, 1921; Vols. II-V, Romae: Jus Pontificium, 1922-1927), III, 110. (Hereafter cited as *Commentaria Minora.*) The territory subject to the jurisdiction of the council includes the territory of those who are affiliated with the province according to the norm of canon 285: "Episcopi qui nulli Metropolitae subiiciuntur, Abbates vel Praelati *nullius*, et Archiepiscopi Suffraganeis carentes, aliquem viciniorem Metropolitam, nisi forte iam elegerint, semel pro semper, praevia Sedis Apostolicae approbatione, eligant, cuius Concilio provinciali cum aliis intersint, et quae ibi ordinata fuerint, observent et observanda curent."

[9] Canon 290. Judicial and coactive aspects of provincial conciliar jurisdiction are greatly restricted in the present law. Cf., e. g., canons 1557, § 1, and 2227, § 1.

[10] Cf. Suarez, *De Legibus et Legislatore Deo*, Lib. VI, cap. 15, nn. 7, 8 (hereafter cited as *De Legibus*)—*Opera Omnia* (28 vols., ed. Vivès, Parisiis, 1856-1861), Vols. V, VI, *De Legibus et Legislatore Deo;* Chelodi, *Ius de Personis*, p. 392; Toso, *Commentaria Minora*, III, 111; Benedictus XIV, *De Syn.*, Lib. XIII, cap. 5, n. 8; cf. *infra*, pp. 35-43.

[11] Cf. Vermeersch-Creusen, *Epitome Iuris Canonici* (3 vols., Mechliniae-Romae: Dessain, Vol. I, 6. ed., 1937; Vol. II, 6. ed., 1940; Vol. III, 5. ed., 1936), I, 315 (hereafter cited as *Epitome*); Fagnanus, Lib. V, tit. 1, cap. 25, n. 87.

[12] *Normae Generales Juris Canonici* (2 vols., Lublin: Universitas Catholica, 1929), I, 503. (Hereafter cited as *Normae Generales.*)

laws, unless the general law contains an express contrary provision.[13] According to this opinion, a general law as described in canon 22 means not only the universal law of the Church but also any other law which is "more general" than another, in the sense that it is of higher rank than the law which is more particular, as, for instance, the laws of plenary councils in relation to the laws of provincial councils, or provincial laws in relation to diocesan statutes.

But this opinion does not appear to be tenable. According to Van Hove,[14] nowhere does the Code use the term "general law" in the alleged sense of "a more general law." Moreover, so Van Hove contends, the reason underlying the prescription of canon 22 is that the supreme legislator cannot be expected to know all the statutes of particular localities, and therefore, unless he expressly states otherwise, he is not presumed to abolish particular laws of which he is not aware. But this reason is not applicable to particular councils, where the ordinaries who enact the laws are considered to know the laws of their own dioceses. Finally, if diocesan statutes could remain firm in opposition to provincial laws, it would appear to contradict the higher law of canon 291, § 2, which absolutely decrees that the laws of particular councils have binding force in the entire territory which is subject to the council, and that the ordinaries cannot dispense except in particular cases and for a just cause.[15]

C. Component Members

At a conciliar assembly, some persons attend to give counsel and are described as having a consultative vote. For the sake of clarity, however, only those who have a deliberative vote at the council will be referred to as members of the council.

[13] Canon 22: . . . firmo praescripto can. 6, n. 1, lex generalis nullatenus derogat locorum specialium et personarum singularium statutis, nisi aliud ipsa expresse caveatur.

[14] *Commentarium Lovaniense in Codicem Iuris Canonici,* Vol. I, Tom. II, *De Legibus Ecclesiasticis,* (Mechliniae-Romae: Dessain, 1930), p. 356 (hereafter cited as *De Legibus*).

[15] Van Hove, *loc. cit.*

The essential elements of a validly constituted provincial council are twofold:

(1) The metropolitan or one who lawfully takes his place must convoke and preside at the council.[16]

(2) Other members, with a deliberative vote, must attend and concur with the metropolitan in the decrees. The presence of persons with a consultative vote is helpful and commanded by law, but their absence would not invalidate the council.[17]

At this point two questions may be asked concerning a validly constituted council: (1) Must there be a quorum or a certain percentage of the bishops of the province present? (2) Is there a minimum number of bishops required by law?

The law does not contain positive specifications on either of these points. In fact, it must be said that the law does not contemplate the situation in which only a minority of the members would attend. The tenor of the present law is to stress positively the obligation of the metropolitan to convoke the council, and the obligation of the suffragan bishops and of others with a decisive vote to attend the council personally. This obligation will appear more clearly when it is shown that a proxy, with a single exception,[18] does not enjoy a deliberative vote at the council. It should, therefore, be the serious concern of each member bishop to attend the council and to assist in the fashioning of the decrees.

Concerning the second question, which speculatively, if not practically, appears to be the more difficult one, the following arguments (tentatively drawn up and then to be evaluated) may be adduced as favoring the requirement that at least three members be present for the valid celebration of a council.

[16] Cf. canon 284, 2°; Toso, *Commentaria Minora,* III, 109; Wernz-Vidal, II, 680.

[17] Cf. canons 290; 286, §§ 3, 4; 287, § 2; Wernz-Vidal, II, 680, 681.

[18] Canon 282, § 1, states that a bishop can send his coadjutor or auxiliary as a proxy, with a decisive vote.

1. Are at Least Three Members Required?

a. Argument from the Analogy of the Council to a Collegiate Moral Person

The legal axiom, *tres faciunt collegium,*[19] has been canonized by the Code so far as all collegiate moral persons are concerned.[20] It seems that provincial councils have a certain analogy to collegiate moral persons, but relative to the point of showing such an analogy it is extremely important to clarify the concepts of a collegiate moral person and a *collegium.* A collegiate moral person is a juridical entity, to which by a formal concession the law attributes a juristic personality, perpetual by nature, existing independently of the physical persons who unite to form it, and possessing the rights and obligations of a single legal person.[21] In early Roman law usage, the term *collegium* meant any organization of persons who were united for a common purpose. Its application did not extend to a collegiate moral person, since in this early period of Roman jurisprudence the concept of juristic personality had not yet evolved. "The name [*collegium*] was retained, however, when these organizations did become juristic persons and was eventually referable to all private and quasi-public corporations." [22] Brown demonstrates that a *collegium* is regarded in law as one person, that it is identified with the concept of a corporation or, in canonical parlance, with a collegiate moral person.[23] The identity of the terms *collegium,* collegiate

[19] Cf. Schmalzgrueber, *Jus Ecclesiasticum Universum* (5 vols. in 12, Romae, 1843-1845), Lib. I, tit. 6, n. 8 (hereafter cited as Schmalzgrueber); D. (50.16) 85.

[20] Canon 100, § 2: Persona moralis collegialis constitui non potest, nisi ex tribus saltem personis physicis.

[21] Maroto, *Institutiones Iuris Canonici ad Normam Novi Codicis* (2 vols., Matriti, Romae, Barcinone, 1918-1919), I, 536 (hereafter cited as *Inst.*): ". . . persona moralis . . . definiri potest: ens iuridicum, independenter a personis singularibus ex concessione iuris subsistens atque capacitate iuris acquirendi exercendique donatum."

[22] Brown, *The Canonical Juristic Personality with Special Reference to Its Status in the United States of America,* The Catholic University of America Canon Law Studies, n. 39 (Washington, D. C.: The Catholic University of America, 1927), p. 14. (Hereafter cited as *Canonical Juristic Personality.*)

[23] *Canonical Juristic Personality,* pp. 18, 47, 65, 78, 79.

person, collegiate moral person appears also in the common usage of canonists.[24] In the adage, *tres faciunt collegium, collegium* is to be understood in the sense of a collegiate moral person, for in the Roman law's acceptation *collegium* here meant a corporation,[25] and, in the canonical acceptation of the axiom, *collegium* was identified with a collegiate person.[26]

The provincial council is not a collegiate person or a *collegium,* since it lacks a perpetual character, while a moral person is by its nature perpetual.[27] A council convenes, makes its laws, and then adjourns. Its quasi-personality as a legislative agency is not perpetual, but transitory. Moreover, a council is not a moral person for the addtional reason that a moral person must be expressly constituted as such by a prescript of the law or by the formal decree of a competent ecclesiastical authority.[28] But a council is by no means declared a moral person in the law, nor can it be declared such by the metropolitan who convokes the council, since he utterly lacks such power, is merely a *primus inter pares,* and the jurisdictional powers of the council itself are restricted by law to the occasion of the conciliar sessions.[29] Hence the axiom, *tres faciunt collegium,* cannot apply directly to the provincial council, which is not a collegiate person.

That a council resembles a *collegium* is apparent from the superior jurisdictional authority which results from the union of the members. Sometimes authors predicate the term *collegium* of the council in an analogous sense, in order to describe the nature of conciliar juris-

[24] Cf. Michiels, *Principia Generalia de Personis in Ecclesia* (Lublin: Universitas Catholica, 1932), pp. 318, 333 (hereafter cited as *De Personis*); Maroto, *Inst.*, I, 546; Wernz-Vidal, II, 34, 35; Beste, *Introductio in Codicem*, p. 162.

[25] Brown, *Canonical Juristic Personality*, p. 65.

[26] Cf. Schmalzgrueber (Lib. I, tit. 6, n. 8), who indicates that a *collegium* is perpetual by nature, since the rights of all the members can reside in even one surviving member: ". . . ad congregationem, seu collegium initio constituendum tres ut minimum personas requiri; si tamen illud semel sit constitutum, conservari posse collegium, ejusque jura etiam in duobus, immo in uno." Cf. Brown, *ibid.*, p. 86.

[27] Cf. canon 102, § 1.

[28] Cf. canon 100, § 1.

[29] Cf. canons 284; 288; 290.

diction.[30] Toso [31] does not call the provincial council a collegiate moral person, but his application of canon 101, § 1, 1°, to provincial councils could lead an incautious reader to infer that a council and a collegiate person are one and the same.[32] Suarez (1548-1617), however, in his description of the nature of conciliar jurisdiction clearly intimated that his language was to be taken in an analogous sense, and he seemed studiously to avoid the use of the word *collegium* or of the term *persona moralis*.[33] The council's superior jurisdictional power, which is not a mere aggregate of the powers of the individual members, is distinct from each physical member in much the same way that a juristic personality exists superior to, and distinct from, its physical members. Another point of similarity between a council and a collegiate moral person is that a majority vote has always been the determining norm of conciliar decisions.[34]

[30] Cf. Wernz, I, n. 181: "Quae potestas legifera a Romano Pontifice concessa Concilio particulari tanquam collegio sive corpori propria est ideoque a maiore parte licite et valide exercetur; minime vero habenda est tanquam additio quaedam arithmetica iurisdictionis singulorum Episcoporum." (That the author is speaking analogously may be inferred from his use of the word *tanquam*.) *Cf.* Chelodi, *Ius de Personis*, p. 392: "Cum autem constet eiusmodi esse naturam iuris in concilio particulari conditi, tenere oportet *collegio* competere peculiarem et superiorem potestatem, quae minime *summa* potestatum eorum qui intersunt est, sed a *iure* ei confertur."

[31] *Commentaria Minora*, III, 110: "Modus autem decernendi cum nihil peculiariter iure communi statuatur, desumendus esse videtur a regula generali de actibus personarum moralium collegialium."

[32] Cf. *infra*, note 37.

[33] *De Legibus*, Lib. VI, cap. 15, n. 4: "Nihilominus respectu singulorum Episcoporum certum est illas leges censeri leges a superiori latas, et ita solum posse in illis dispensare quatenus illis concessum est expresse, vel tacite vel consuetudine. Ratio est, quia revera in Concilio provinciali, ut est unum corpus mysticum, est vera jurisdictio quasi per se una moraliter (ut sic rem explicem), et non tantum est aggregatum iurisdictionum."

[34] Cf. *supra*, p. 18, note 106; cf. canon 101, § 1, 1°, which provides similarly for the acts of collegiate persons. (One could adduce the argument that the mere fact that a majority vote is required at provincial councils indicates that at least three persons are to be present as members. It is true, indeed, that the first connotation of the expression, "majority vote," seems to imply that more than a mere plurality of persons be at hand. Still, if only two attending members were in accord, the exigencies of attaining a majority vote would be satisfied.)

Scherer (1845-1918)[35] stated that it seemed better to require the presence of at least the metropolitan, who convoked the council, and of two other members. In connection with this statement he made an indirect reference to the axiom, *tres faciunt collegium,* in support of his view.[36] Toso[37] also regards the requirement of at least three members as apparently essential for a provincial council, on the grounds that general principles must be applied to solve the present question. The author employs the argument based upon the analogy of a provincial council to a collegiate moral person.

[35] *Handbuch des Kirchenrechtes* (2 vols., Graz-Leipzig, 1886-1898), I, p. 674, note 24.

[36] *Ibid.,* p. 576, note 41. Wernz-Vidal (II, p. 681, note 44) stated the following concerning the opinion of Scherer: ". . . Scherer . . . *praeter* praesidem, Concilium provinciale convocantem, tantum duos alios Praelatos voto decisivo praeditos absolute *requiri* et sufficere ex(s)istimat, sed argumentis allatis non demonstrat . . ." The position of Wernz-Vidal is not quite clear, but they seemed to object to Scherer's view on the grounds that he absolutely required three members, since they italicized the word *requiri,* and they also rejected the opinion that a majority of the members was required for the validity of the council. Cf. *infra,* pp. 41, 42.

[37] *Commentaria Minora,* III, 109: "Sed quid de numero intervenientium? Sane videntur nobis principia generalia esse applicanda, nempe: (1) Omnes, ad convocationis validitatem, legitime invitari oportere; (2) Ad Patres, qui praesentes sunt, ius agendi spectare, dummodo cum praeside ternarium saltem numerum efficiant, qui procul dubio requiritur, uti collegium legitime agere possit (cf. can. 101, § 1, et 163)." From the author's concluding clause one could readily draw the mistaken inference that a provincial council and a collegiate moral person are one and the same. Moreover, the author's reference to canons 101, § 1, and 163, does not, in the mind of the present writer, conclusively demonstrate that at least three persons are required for the legitimate *acts* of collegiate moral persons. (So far as the terms of canon 101, § 1, are concerned, the requirement of attaining an absolute majority vote would seem to be satisfied if only two attending members of a *collegium* voted concordantly. Cf. Coronata, *Inst.,* I, 158 and *ibid.,* note 1; Maroto, *Inst.,* I, 552.) It seems more precise to place the argument of analogy on the following basis: just as at least three persons are required to *constitute* a collegiate moral person (cf. canon 100, § 2), so at least three members should be required to constitute a provincial council.

b. Argument from Other Analogies of Law

An argument of analogy may be alleged from the practice of the Roman Curia. In the Roman Congregations at least three cardinals are required for a plenary session, so that if only two cardinals are present they cannot conduct the matter at hand without securing authorization from the Holy Father.[38]

A group of three or more persons is an aptly constituted group, and is often determined in law where important decisions are to be made. Thus, tribunals on certain weighty matters require at least three judges.[39] The law provides for the judgment or counsel of three or more persons in the administrative processes for the transfer and removal of pastors,[40] and in the institution of the *consilium administrationis*,[41] of the *consilium missionis*[42] and of the diocesan consultors.[43]

From these many analogies of law and in view of the gravity and importance of provincial legislation, which governs a large ecclesiastical territory, it seems fitting that the enacting of such laws should result from the judgment of at least three local ordinaries.

c. Argument from the Practice of Provincial Councils

As a matter of historical fact, councils with less than three members must be termed a non-entity, or at least a rarity if, indeed, examples of such councils (unknown to the writer) may be alleged.[44]

[38] Wernz-Vidal (II, p. 680, note 44) suggested this argument, but apparently did not regard it as conclusive in the present question, since they rejected the position of Scherer.

[39] Cf. canons 1576, § 1, 1°; 1572, § 2; 1596.

[40] Cf. canons 2165; 2148; 2159.

[41] Cf. canon 1520, § 1.

[42] Cf. canon 302.

[43] Cf. canon 425, which requires as a bare minimum four consultors.

[44] Cf. Hinschius (III, p. 640, note 3), who stated that the question concerning the number of bishops required for a provincial council did not arise, since in practice the metropolitan did not convoke councils unless a good attendance of suffragans could be expected. Cf. also *Glossa ordinaria*, c. 1, C. XV, q. 7, ad v. *Concilii*: "Ergo tres episcopi faciunt concilium: quia tres episcopi examinant causam diaconi." The twelfth century commentator on

d. Criticism of the Three Preceding Arguments

The presented arguments are not to be dismissed lightly. It appears that, if a provincial council were to be celebrated with only two voting members at hand, the Holy See's authorization should be secured before these would proceed to the celebration of the council. For the likeness of a provincial council to a true collegiate body, the practice of the Sacred Congregations, and also the invariable practice of the councils themselves would apparently, according to canon 20, dictate the norm that at least three members should be present to constitute the legislative body which is described in canon 290. It must be admitted, however, that not only is the law itself silent concerning the requirement of a minimum number of members for a conciliar gathering, but also there have existed provinces consisting of only two sees, such as those of Besançon,[45] Cambrai,[46] Gniezno-Posnan [47] and Cardiff.[48]

Hinschius (1835-1898) [49] reasoned that, since provinces such as these were true provinces, true provincial councils could be held,

Gratian's *Decretum* made this inference from the comparison he instituted between c. 1, C. XV, q. 7, which required a council for the trial of a deacon, and c. 3, C. XV, q. 7, which required three bishops for the trial of a deacon. It is to be noted, however, that the Glossator spoke only as a private teacher, and that his inference was based, not on articles of the universal law of the Church, but on the two following sources of particular law: can. 6, II Council of Seville (618): ". . . decrevimus ut juxta priscorum patrum synodalem sententiam nullus nostrum sine concilii examine deiiciendum quemlibet . . . diaconum audeat . . ."—Bruns, II, 70 (this is substantially the same as c. 1, C. XV, q. 7); can. 11, I Council of Carthage (348): ". . . a tribus vicinis episcopis si diaconus est arguatur . . ."—Bruns, I, 115 (this text is closely similar to c. 3, C. XV, q. 7).

[45] Cf. Gams, *Series Episcoporum Ecclesiae Catholicae* (2 vols. in 1, Ratisbonae, 1873-1886), I, 475 (hereafter cited as *Series Episcoporum*).

[46] *Ibid.*, p. 476.

[47] *Ibid.*, p. 257.

[48] Cf. *The Official Catholic Directory* (4 parts, Part IV, *The Catholic Church in Ireland, England, Scotland, Wales, Cuba and Mexico*, New York: Kenedy, 1946), Part IV, pp. 51, 97. The province of Cardiff (Wales) was erected with one suffragan on February 7, 1916.

[49] *Das Kirchenrecht der Katholiken und Protestanten in Deutschland*, III, p. 640, note 4.

provided that the two member bishops could come to agreement upon the decrees. It seems that the point is well taken, for the tacit permission of the Holy See appears to be present in such a case for celebrating the provincial council, to which all metropolitans are bound by the common law.[50] Likewise it cannot be said that if a province has only two sees their decrees in a council would be equivalent to merely diocesan statutes, for neither bishop could dispense from the provincial laws (as he could from diocesan statutes), except in particular cases and for a just cause.[51]

Apart from the extraordinary circumstance of a province consisting of an archdiocese and only one suffragan see, it seems that the authorization of the Holy See should be secured for the celebrating of a council which consists of less than three members.[52]

One may project the following case. In a province consisting of three sees, two members and a procurator who lacks a decisive vote attend a legitimately convoked council. Can it be asserted absolutely that the acts and decrees of such a council are invalid? *Post factum,* the writer would hesitate to make such an assertion, since a positive and clear determination of invalidity does not appear to be contained in the law.[53]

[50] Metropolitans, who have at least one suffragan (cf. canon 272), are distinguished from archbishops who lack suffragans (cf. canon 285: . . . Archiepiscopi Suffraganeis carentes . . .). Cf. canons 283, 284, concerning the obligation of metropolitans to convoke provincial councils. Cf. Beste (*Introductio in Codicem,* p. 252) concerning canon 272.

[51] Cf. canons 82; 291, § 2.

[52] Provincial councils consisting of only two prelates appear to be something of an anomaly. The Holy See's attitude in this matter is reflected in the provision, made in 1919, that certain regions of Italy, where the provinces were small or lacked suffragans, should combine and celebrate plenary councils, instead of provincial councils, within each period of twenty years. Cf. S. C. Consist., 15 febr. 1919—*Acta Apostolicae Sedis, Commentarium Officiale* (Romae, 1909—), XI (1919), 72-74 (hereafter cited as *AAS*); S. C. Consist., 22 mart. 1919—*AAS,* XI (1919), 175-177.

[53] Canon 11: Irritantes aut inhabilitantes eae tantum leges habendae sunt, quibus aut actum esse nullum aut inhabilem esse personam expresse vel aequivalenter statuitur. Canon 15: Leges, etiam irritantes et inhabilitantes, in dubio iuris non urgent . . . Scherer (*Handbuch des Kirchenrechtes,* I, p. 674, note 24) admitted that his opinion, which required the presence of three members, could well meet with contradiction in practice.

2. Is a Quorum Required?

With all the more reason and security should the doubt concerning the necessity of a quorum of the bishops for the celebrating of a council yield to the fact that the law contains no such positive requirement. While Wernz (1842-1914)-Vidal (1867-1938) [54] asserted that the presence of two-thirds of the total number of bishops suffices for a legitimately constituted council, this assertion does not imply, as at first it might appear, that a smaller percentage of attendance is thereby declared inadequate. Wernz-Vidal reasoned that, since the law is not express on the point concerning the required percentage of membership at a council, there should be invoked the analogy of this case with that of cathedral chapters and of religious orders, as governed by the norm of canon 162, § 3. It must be observed, however, that this canon does not declare invalid an electoral assembly at which less than two-thirds of the members are present, but rather declares an election null only then when more than one-third of the members were passed by and not informed, when the invitation and call to the election should have included them.[55] The point at issue, then, in this canon is not a requirement of the presence of two-thirds of the membership, but rather (as the next paragraph of the canon words it), a "defect of convocation." [56]

Wernz-Vidal [57] themselves did not give credence to the view of Sägmüller (1860-1942) [58] and Hinschius [59] that at least a majority of the members was required for the validity of the celebration of a provincial council. Hinschius admitted that no positive disposition of law could be advanced for his opinion, but he argued, from the nature of the case, that the province should be represented by the

[54] *Ius Canonicum,* II, 680.

[55] Canon 162, § 3: Quod si plures quam tertia pars electorum neglecti fuerint, electio est ipso iure nulla.

[56] Canon 162, § 4: *Defectus convocationis* non obstat, si praetermissi nihilominus interfuerint. (Emphasis added.)

[57] *Ius Canonicum,* II, 680, note 44.

[58] *Lehrbuch des Katholischen Kirchenrechts* (2 vols., 3. ed., Freiburg im Breisgau, 1914), I, 502.

[59] *Das Kirchenrecht der Katholiken und Protestanten in Deutschland,* III, p. 640, note 4.

bishops who constituted it, since otherwise a minority of the bishops could impose laws upon the majority. Wernz-Vidal [60] and Scherer [61] replied to this argument that *a priori* constructed arguments did not prove the point at issue, since otherwise it could be stated *a pari* that an ecumenical council could not be validly celebrated unless a majority of the bishops of the whole Church were actually present, which latter doctrine would be a plainly false one.

In summary, the solution of the present question looks to the guiding norms which are derived from analogies of law and from the practice of the provincial councils. These guiding norms may be stated briefly thus: it would be rash to assert that less than three members can constitute a council if the Holy See's permission is lacking; but there appears no compelling proof that more than three members are required as a condition for validity.

D. Decisions of the Council

In the provincial council, unlike plenary and ecumenical councils,[62] all important decisions and even certain points of procedure, such as the order of business, the opening and adjournment of the council, its transfer or prolongation, are determined, not by the presiding officer, but by the consent of the members. However, previously to the actual celebration of the council, the metropolitan alone, or, if a lawful impediment prevents him, the *suffraganeus antiquior* (i.e. the bishop who was first appointed a suffragan of the province) has the exclusive right and duty of convoking the council. The consent of the suffragan bishops is not involved here. Moreover, in the selection of the place for the council, the metropolitan, while bound to consult the reasons for the choice of the suffragan bishops,[63] still has the power to decide against their choice. Again, a majority vote does not rule in this instance.[64] Finally, the office of presiding at the council (which office is proper to the metropolitan or to his

[60] *Ius Canonicum, loc. cit.*

[61] *Handbuch des Kirchenrechtes,* I, p. 674, note 24.

[62] Canons 288; 222, § 2.

[63] Cf. canon 105, 1° and 2°; cf. *infra*, pp. 86-88.

[64] Canon 284, 1°.

legitimate substitute, as already described) is conferred by the law, and does not depend upon the consent of the bishops.[65]

With these exceptions, namely, the right of convoking the council, of selecting the place for its celebration, and of presiding at its sessions, the metropolitan and suffragan bishops share equally in all conciliar decisions and decrees, which are determined by a majority vote of the assembled members. The requirement of a majority vote is not specified explicitly in the common law, but it has remained through the centuries as a stable element of the provincial council's constitution,[66] and resembles to some extent the general canonical norms which are defined for the actions of collegiate moral persons, as determined in canon 101, § 1, 1°. However, an essential distinction must be made. As noted above, the council is not a collegiate moral person,[67] and the metropolitan, as the president of the council, is only a *"primus inter pares."* His vote does not exceed in any respect the vote of any other member. He does not possess the power, by virtue of canon 101, § 1, 1°, as does the president of a collegiate moral person, to exercise any additional influence, or to cast a further vote in order to remove a tie. Moreover, a relative majority vote does not suffice for the determining of conciliar enactments. Whenever, therefore, the law demands the consent of the assembled prelates, it is always an absolute majority vote that is required.[68]

Article 2. Limitations of Power

A. Laws of a Higher Legislative Superior

There is in the Church a hierarchy of jurisdiction[69] and, as a consequence, there is also a hierarchy of laws. It would be not

[65] Canon 284, 2°.

[66] Cf. *supra,* p. 18, note 106; Suarez, *De Legibus,* Lib. VI, cap. 15, n. 6: ". . . talis est jurisdictio Concilii provincialis ut actus ejus communi consensu, seu maioris partis fieri debeant . . ." Cf. canon 286, § 2.

[67] Cf. *supra,* p. 35.

[68] Cf. *supra,* in the present Chapter, note 66.

[69] Canon 108, § 3: Ex divina institutione sacra hierarchia . . . constat . . . ratione iurisdictionis pontificatu supremo et episcopatu subordinato; ex Ecclesiae autem institutione alii quoque gradus accessere.

only unlawful, but also invalid, for a legislator of intermediate status to invade the jurisdiction of his own legislative superior, and to countermand his decrees, for otherwise the whole hierarchical structure of the Church would be undermined. Moreover, as Suarez pointed out,[70] the right of contravening a superior's laws would imply that in its effective use, the superior's power depended upon that of his inferior, which implication is altogether inadmissible. The council, as noted above, possesses a jurisdictional authority which is superior to the episcopal power as such and which is derived from a grant of the Church. One of the precise objects of this concession of jurisdictional power is to secure the more exact and uniform observance of the general laws of the Church.[71] Provincial decrees which would contradict the law of legislative superior would obviously be *ipso facto* invalid, since competent authority would be lacking.[72]

1. Prescriptions of the Present Code

Under the general term "prescriptions" are here included a twofold division of law as commonly delineated by canonists, namely, affirmative and negative laws.[73] This division is helpful for the attainment of a clearer perception of the ways in which a lawgiver of lower rank, that is, of intermediate status, might legislate invalidly by opposing an existing law enacted by his legislative superior. The sources of such a contradiction could be the following:

(1) Affirmative or preceptive laws, which command an act; and
(2) Negative or prohibitive laws, which forbid an action.

(1) It would be invalid for the legislative inferior to forbid the act which a higher authority commands; he cannot abrogate the law

[70] *De Legibus*, Lib. VI, cap. 26, n. 4.

de accusationibus, inquisitionibus, et denunciationibus, V, 1.

[71] Can. 6, IV Council of the Lateran (1215)—Mansi, XXII, 991; c. 25, X,

[72] Cf. Suarez, *loc. cit.*; *cf.* also canon 22, which postulates the necessity of competent authority in the legislator for the abrogation of law, and canon 335, § 1, which requires a bishop to conform to the norms of the sacred canons in the exercise of his powers.

[73] Michiels, *Normae Generales*, I, 252.

of his legislative superior. Also invalid would be preceptive laws even if they were only indirectly repugnant or in virtual contradiction to the law of the legislative superior by commanding an act whose performance would make the observance of the superior's law impossible.[74]

(2) The inferior authority cannot licitly or validly command disobedience. He cannot command what his superior forbids.

In the Code of Canon Law certain matters are expressly reserved to the supreme legislative authority. Matters affecting the universal discipline of the Church, such as the institution of feast days and days of fast and abstinence,[75] the institution of irregularities affecting candidates for sacred orders [76] and the definition or institution of matrimonial impediments (whether diriment or prohibitive),[77] all being exclusively to the jurisdiction of the Holy See.

2. Permissive Regulations of the Present Code

Permissive regulations of the Code, as limiting the field of conciliar legislation, are only those which constitute permissive laws understood in the strict sense. A permissive law in the broad sense is one which simply omits mention of a certain point, with the result that there is a merely implicit concession to the liberty of the subject. In other words, when the law fails to prohibit some act it does not thereby decree a legal permission, since, in point of fact, the legislator has not acted to manifest his will.[78] Such matters, designated as being *praeter ius,* can become the subject matter of provincial enactments.

It is only in regard to permissive laws taken in the strict sense that the question arises of a possible conflict with the law of a legis-

[74] Suarez, *De Legibus*, Lib. VI, cap. 27, n. 2.

[75] Cf. canon 1244.

[76] Canon 983.

[77] Canon 1038.

[78] Cf. Donnelly, *The Diocesan Synod,* The Catholic University of America Canon Law Studies, n. 74, (Washington, D. C.: The Catholic University of America, 1932), p. 94.

lative superior. Permissive laws understood in the strict sense are those which positively and expressly confer a certain concession, which is decreed and stabilized by the law. Such laws limit the legislative inferior in that he cannot validly contravene the positive permission granted by his superior.[79]

For example, all priests are given the express permission by the Code for the celebration of three Masses on Christmas Day.[80] A provincial council could not curtail this concession of the common law. Another example, actually drawn into controversy since the promulgation of the Code, involves canon 838. This canon clearly gives priests the right to transfer Masses, even outside the diocese, provided that the free disposal of them is not limited by the donor. The Sacred Congregation of the Council, on February 19, 1921, declared that a provincial enactment forbidding the transfer of such Masses outside the diocese without the permission of the ordinary was contrary to the Code.[81]

Also invalid, it seems, would be a provincial enactment that visiting priests, in order to celebrate Mass, must present a testimonial letter issued by the local chancery in addition to the *celebret* already issued by their own proper ordinary. This would conflict with canon 804, § 1, which confers a positive right, namely, that testimonial letters from one's proper ordinary (or from one's religious superior or the Sacred Congregation for the Oriental Church, as the case demands) are a title, which must be recognized, for the right to offer Mass.[82]

It may be difficult at times to determine in a concrete case whether a permission is positively conceded by law, or whether it is merely

[79] Michiels, *Normae Generales,* I, 253.

[80] Canon 806, § 1.

[81] *AAS,* XIII (1921), 228-230; Bouscaren, *The Canon Law Digest* (2 vols., Milwaukee: Bruce, 1934-1943), I, 399, 400 (hereafter cited as Bouscaren). This decision stated that the decree of the council was to have force only with regard to founded Masses, Masses *ad instar manualium,* and manual Masses which were given for the benefit of a pious cause, since such Masses are not at the priest's free disposal.

[82] Michiels, *Normae Generales,* I, 256.

a point upon which the law remains silent. Whenever a *dubium iuris* exists, the legislative inferior is not restricted, since a doubtful law does not bind.[83]

Any provincial decree opposed to the privileges and exemptions granted to religious by the Holy Father or by the common law would of course be invalid.[84] But the conciliar assembly should not omit consideration of the needs for legislation in those matters in which religious are subject to the local ordinary.[85]

3. Particular Laws of the Holy See

Laws which the Holy Father has decreed for a particular territory emanate from the supreme legislative authority and have the same force in that territory as the laws of the Code.[86] It is to be observed that the decrees of the Roman Congregations which are issued for a certain territory are particular laws of the Holy See,[87] since the Sacred Congregation possesses vicarious power, which is exercised in the name and authority of the Pope. Their decrees, therefore, supersede the enactments of provincial councils.

4. Decrees of a Plenary Council

Plenary councils possess a higher and a more extensive jurisdiction than that of provincial councils.[88] As is indicated in canon 281, a plenary council requires for its celebration the permission of the Holy Father and it also presupposes that the Holy Father's own legate convoke the council and preside over it. It is thus distin-

[83] Canon 15: Leges, etiam irritantes et inhabilitantes, in dubio iuris non urgent . . .

[84] Benedictus XIV, *De Syn.*, Lib. IX, cap. 15, n. 1.

[85] Benedictus XIV, *ibid.*, n. 4.

[86] Canon 82 requires the same norms for dispensations from particular laws of the Holy See as from the general laws of the Code.

[87] Reilly, *The General Norms of Dispensation*, The Catholic University of America Canon Law Studies, n. 119 (Washington, D. C.: The Catholic University of America Press, 1939), p. 91.

[88] Toso, *Commentaria Minora*, III, 110.

guished from the provincial council, not only in the more intimate participation in its proceedings on the part of the Holy See and in its higher authority, but also in the fact that its laws bind more than one province. It is worthy of note that it is not required that all the provinces of a nation participate in a council before such a council can rightfully be designated as a plenary council. Any council which embraces more than one province and is at the same time less than an ecumenical (general) council of the Church is a plenary council.[89]

Those who are to take part in a provincial council should, therefore, consult the decrees of the plenary councils which govern their territory, both to urge their support and to forestall any conflict with the laws enacted through their higher legislative authority.

B. Recognitio *of Conciliar Decrees*

Canon 291, § 1. Absoluto Concilio . . . provinciali, praeses acta et decreta omnia ad Sanctam Sedem transmittat, nec eadem antea promulgentur, quam a Sacra Congregatione Concilii expensa et recognita fuerint . . .

The practice of submitting provincial conciliar enactments to reconsideration and review on the part of the Holy See is not a new one. It became part of the universal law of the Church in the year 1588 through the Constitution "*Immensa aeterni*" of Pope Sixtus V.[90]

The presiding officer of the council is required to send the acts and decrees, bearing the signatures of all the Fathers of the council, for official review by the Holy See.[91] The law states that before their promulgation the conciliar acts and decrees are to be sent for

[89] Toso, *ibid.*, p. 103. The territory which is governed by plenary legislation is usually, but not necessarily, coterminous with a nation. The special instructions of the Holy See specify which provinces are to participate in the plenary council, when one is to be celebrated. Cf. Wernz-Vidal, II, 676.

[90] *Bull. Rom. Taur.*, VIII, 991.

[91] Even those members who in the deliberations voted in the dissenting minority affix their signatures to the decrees, since the enactments will have

examination and supervision (*recognitio*) by the Sacred Congregation of the Council.[92]

The reserving of this official supervision (*recognitio*) imports the right of the Holy See to examine the acts and decrees of the council, in order to test their validity, to weigh their wisdom and prudence, and to make any corrections which may be desirable. The Sacred Congregation's appraisal of the proceedings and enactments constitutes an additional safeguard in the framing of a uniform provincial law which will not be too rigid or out of harmony with that mildness of spirit which is termed canonical equity. But it is to be carefully noted that even if the Sacred Congregation makes additions to the measures submitted, this does not imply a change in the intrinsic nature of the decrees. Censorship and correction by the Holy See do not give the decrees a pontifical authority, nor do they receive thereby a positive ratification.[93] Thus, if the conciliar enactments contain anything opposed to the common law, they lack juridical force, despite the official supervision accorded to them. Such invalidity, however, is not to be presumed, but would have to be proved.[94] In other words, the *recognitio* of the Sacred Congregation of the Council confers only an extrinsic, not an intrinsic, author-

force in the whole province. Cf. Benedictus XIV, *De Syn.*, Lib. XIII, cap. 2, n. 4; Fagnanus, Lib. V, tit. 1, cap. 25, n. 94; Cocchi, *Commentarium in Codicem Iuris Canonici* (8 vols. in 5, Vol. III, 3. ed. recognita, Taurinorum Augustae: Marietti, 1931), III, 135. (Hereafter cited as *Commentarium.*)

[92] Coronata (*Inst.*, I, p. 424, note 7) remarks that the statutes are examined by one consultor, then by all the consultors (or at least five consultors), and finally by all the Cardinals of the Congregation.

Cf. canon 304, § 2, which states that in Mission places which are subject to the Sacred Congregation for the Propagation of the Faith it is that Congregation which exercises the office of supervising the conciliar acts and decrees.

[93] "Namque approbatio S. Sedis quae mere condicio est legitimae promulgationis, nullam positivam S. Sedis auctoritatem ad ista decreta superaddit."—S. C. C., 19 febr. 1921—*AAS*, XIII (1921), 228. *Recognitio* does not imply approbation even *in forma communi*. Cf. Chelodi, *Ius de Personis*, p. 393.

[94] Coronata, *Inst.*, I, p. 424, note 7.

ity upon the decrees.[95] Certainly the fact of supervision and review by the Holy See gives to the decrees an added importance and solemnity, and furthers their ready acceptance and prompt execution among both the clergy and the laity.[96]

A doubt may be raised as to whether the present canon (291, § 1) states clearly enough that any attempt at the promulgation of conciliar decrees without the required *recognitio* would be not only unlawful but also invalid. The canon first states a positive command, enjoining upon the presiding officer the obligation of transmitting all the acts and decrees to the Holy See, and then states a prohibition, forbidding the promulgation of the decrees before the Sacred Congregation of the Council has examined and reviewed them. Of itself, such a command together with the prohibition does not appear to contain an express or equivalent declaration of invalidity.[97]

Vermeersch-Creusen,[98] in their commentary on canon 11, hold that an equivalent expression of invalidity is found only where the

[95] A provincial council, held in China in 1924, had incorporated in its decrees, which subsequently had also been accorded the requisite official *recognitio*, a point on implicit dispensation, touching on canon 1071, in a manner which proved to be at variance with the practice of the Holy Office. Eight years later, in a private reply sent to the Apostolic Delegation in China, on June 30, 1932, the Holy Office ordered that this particular decree should be corrected. Cf. Sartori, *Enchiridion Canonicum* (3. ed., emendata et aucta [1917-1932] Hankow: Missio Catholica, 1932), p. 146; Bouscaren, II, 291, 292; *ibid.*, I, 512, 513; Hanrahan, "The Law on Plenary Councils"—*The Clergy Review*, XIV (1938), 387-402, 401; "From Foreign Reviews"—*The Clergy Review*, XIV (1938), 89, 90.

[96] Wernz-Vidal, II, 684. If the Holy Father should give to the decrees his personal approbation *in forma specifica* (*motu proprio et ex certa scientia*), they would obtain the force of pontifical laws, but such approbation is not often given. Cf. Oesterle, *Praelectiones Iuris Canonici* (Vol. I, Romae: In Collegio S. Anselmi, 1931), I, 157. The force of such pontifical laws would not extend beyond the limits of the given province, unless the Pope expressly stated otherwise. Cf. Benedictus XIV, *De Syn.*, Lib. XIII, cap. 3, n. 5.

[97] Canon 11: Irritantes aut inhabilitantes eae tantum leges habendae sunt, quibus aut actum esse nullum aut inhabilem esse personam expresse vel aequivalenter statuitur.

[98] *Epitome*, I, 101.

very words of the law have some reference to invalidity, as in the expression, "diriment impediment." They, and with them a host of approved authors,[99] explain the term *"aequivalenter"* in canon 11 as requiring that the text of the law itself must contain some verbal expression which is tantamount to an express declaration of nullity, such as *"effectum non sortitur,"* [100] *"nullum habet iuridicum effectum,"* [101] *"nihil est actum."* [102]

It could be contended that in canon 291, § 1, the prohibition of the promulgation is tantamount to an exclusion of the promulgation, which is essential for a law's institution.[103] However, in the opinion of the writer, the conclusive argument for the invalidating force of the clause in question arises from the fact that it forms a part of the constitutive common law affecting the provincial council,[104] and accordingly should be interpreted in the light of the former law,[105] since canon 291, § 1, does not express any change in the matter.[106]

Pre-Code authors regarded the called for *recognitio* as an indispensable element of conciliar law and as a *conditio sine qua non* for the effective promulgation of conciliar decrees.[107] Authors since

[99] Wernz-Vidal, I, 217: "Aequivalenter statuitur, si lex inducat impedimentum dirimens; si absolute sanciat hoc vel illud *fieri nequit . . ."*; Van Hove, *De Legibus,* p. 168; Michiels, *Normae Generales,* I, 276, 277; Toso, *Commentaria Minora,* I, 36; Beste, *Introductio in Codicem,* p. 67; Roelker, "The Interpretation of Invalidating Laws"—*The Jurist,* III (1943), 364-403, 377-402. Cf. also canon 1680, § 1.

[100] Cf. canon 116.

[101] Cf. canon 162, § 5.

[102] Cf. canon 171, § 3.

[103] Canon 8, § 1: Leges instituuntur, cum promulgantur. Cf. *infra,* pp. 116-119, concerning the promulgation of conciliar decrees.

[104] Wernz-Vidal, II, 673; *Bull. Rom. Taur.,* VIII, 991.

[105] Cf. *supra,* p. 25, note 21.

[106] Cf. canon 6, 2°.

[107] Petra, *Commentaria,* I, p. 284, n. 121: "Et omnes docent, ut transmittantur statuta haec Conciliaria Papae, qui solet ea approbare, medio oraculo Sac. Congreg. Concilii, nec possunt imprimi, aut executioni demandari sine dicta facultate . . . ac est dispositum in Constitutione Sixti V." Cf. also Fagnanus, Lib. V, tit. 1, cap. 25, n. 95; Gousset, *Exposition des Principes du Droit Canonique* (Paris, 1859), p. 296 (hereafter cited as Gousset); Bouix, *De Con-*

the time of the Code's promulgation have retained this position and support the view, maintained by the writer, that without the Holy See's antecedent *recognitio* the promulgation of conciliar decrees would be not only illicit but also invalid.[108]

cilio Provinciali, p. 371; Scherer, *Handbuch des Kirchenrechtes,* I, 674; Wernz, I, p. 265, note 42: "Antequam recognitionem illam factam acta et decreta Concil. partic. promulgari valide non possunt."

[108] Wernz-Vidal, II, 683; Coronata, *Inst.,* I, p. 424, note 8; Chelodi, *Ius de Personis,* p. 393. Toso (*Commentaria Minora,* III, 103, 110) explains the necessity of the fulfillment of this condition of *recognitio* on the part of the Holy See from the nature of the conciliar power, which exceeds the episcopal power as such, and is therefore contingent for its exercise upon the fulfillment of the conditions prescribed by the Holy Father.

CHAPTER IV

OBJECTS AND METHODS OF LEGISLATION

ARTICLE 1. GENERAL OBJECTS OF LEGISLATION

Canon 290. Patres in Concilio . . . provinciali congregati studiose inquirant ac decernant quae ad fidei incrementum, ad moderandos mores, ad corrigendos abusus, ad controversias componendas, ad unam eandemque disciplinam servandam vel inducendam, opportuna fore pro suo cuiusque territorio videantur.

THE Fathers of the council are charged with the obligation of searching out zealously (*studiose inquirant*) matters that call for provincial legislation. The need for such legislation is again indicated in canon 292, § 1. At the episcopal conferences which are to be held in each province at least once within every period of five years, the ordinaries are required to prepare matters for legislation at the next provincial council.

In her wisdom and experience the Church knows that problems of a local nature will inevitably arise. No fixed norm can be determined in advance for coping with the deviations from law that may occur. Hence, the enumeration of the purposes of conciliar decrees, as stated in canon 290, appears to be simply demonstrative rather than absolutely all-inclusive. Moreover, these purposes are not necessarily mutually exclusive. Whatever serves to further a unity of discipline may also well tend toward the furthering of an increase of faith. The correction of abuses will favor uniform discipline. With the exception of the phrase *"ad incrementum fidei"* many of the words of the canon have a familiar ring, echoing time-honored legislation.[1]

[1] Canon 290 resembles strikingly the laws of the Council of Trent (1545-1563) and of the IV Council of the Lateran (1215). Cf. Conc. Trident., sess. XXIV, *de ref.*, c. 2: "Provincialia Concilia, sicubi omissa sunt, pro moderandis moribus, corrigendis excessibus, controversiis componendis aliisque ex sacris canon-

The final clause of canon 290 points to the fact that the opportuneness of provincial decrees is derived from their close connection with local needs. The general laws of the Code look to the provincial council for support. The vigilance and prudence of a legislator who is thoroughly acquainted with local conditions and with the precise pattern that legislation should follow are called for.[2]

A. Increase of Faith and Preservation of Morals

It is not the power to define matters of faith, but the task of promoting the increase of faith that is committed to the provincial council. Matters which are difficult or controverted, whether in faith or in morals, are reserved by their nature to the supreme infallible authority in the Church.[3] Provincial councils, therefore, are not competent to issue definitions in faith or in morals, since provincial councils are not infallible.[4] But they have the important office of issuing disciplinary decrees.

Disciplinary laws are those by which the members of the Church are externally assisted in the profession of their faith and are taught to live in a Christian manner.[5] Disciplinary laws are based upon the already authentically defined or theologically certain teaching

ibus permissis renoventur." Cf. IV Council of the Lateran, can. 6: ". . . provincialia non omittant concilia celebrare, in quibus de corrigendis excessibus et moribus reformandis, praesertim in clero, diligentem habeant cum Dei timore tractatum, canonicas regulas, et maxime, quae statutae sunt in hoc generali concilio, relegentes, ut eas faciant observari, debitam poenam transgressoribus infligendo."—Mansi, XXII, 991; c. 25, X, *de accusationibus, inquisitionibus et denunciationibus,* V, 1.

[2] Benedictus XIV, *De Syn.,* Lib. VI, cap. 3, n. 1: "Audivimus nuper ab Isidoro, legem convenire debere loco et tempori: ex hoc vere illud consequitur, quod iam superius animadvertimus, non posse videlicet certam regulam praescribi, quae Constitutiones indigitet in qualibet Synodo edendas; quae enim uno tempore, atque in uno loco saluberrimae sunt, alio tempore, alioque in loco incassum renovantur."

[3] Cf. canon 1323; cf. also Wernz, I, n. 181; Chelodi, *Ius de Personis,* p. 392; Augustine, *A Commentary on the New Code of Canon Law* (8 vols., Vol. II, St. Louis, 1918; Vol. VI, 2. ed., 1923), II, 305 (hereafter cited as *Commentary*); Fagnanus, Lib. V, tit. 1, cap. 25, n. 82.

[4] Cf. canon 1326.

[5] Vermeersch-Creusen, *Epitome,* I, 18.

of the Church in faith and morals. The assembled prelates, who are constituted as true teachers of the province,[6] will warn against current errors. They will vindicate the Church against her enemies by exposing misrepresentations, by proclaiming the true Catholic doctrine, and by instituting means to publish it among the people.[7] They will likewise point out the dangers to morals and with all zeal will explain, commend and decree whatever will promote the spiritual betterment of a united province.

Especially important for the increase of faith and for the safeguarding of morals are disciplinary regulations for the clergy. Hence the establishment of such regulations should be given a prominent position among the matters before the council.[8] Decrees that favor vocations to the priesthood and to the religious life, and that further the progress of seminaries will have far reaching effects in the moral and religious life of the faithful at large.[9]

B. Correction of Abuses

Abuses, of whatever sort, whether violations of the disciplinary law of the Church or of the divine law, must be met with determination by the conciliar assembly if they are to be stemmed and removed.

[6] Canon 1326: Episcopi quoque, licet singuli vet etiam in Conciliis particularibus congregati infallibilitate docendi non polleant, fidelium tamen suis curis commissorum, sub auctoritate Romani Pontificis, veri doctores seu magistri sunt.

[7] De Meester, *Juris Canonici et Juris Canonico-Civilis Compendium* (ed. nova, 3 vols. in 4, Brugis: Sumptibus et Typis Societatis Sancti Augustini, 1921-1928), II, 115. (Hereafter cited as De Meester.)

[8] Conc. Trident., sess. XXIV, *de ref.*, c. 2; Fagnanus, Lib. V, tit. 1, cap. 25, n. 13.

[9] The Council of Trent (sess. XXIII, *de ref.*, cap. 18) committed to the solicitude of the provincial council the institution and conservation of a seminary in each diocese, or the erecting of at least one seminary in a province, through the united efforts of the bishops, if the dioceses individually could not support a seminary. Cf. Fagnanus, Lib. V, tit. 1, cap. 25, n. 62. Canon 1354 of the Code provides that each diocese shall have its own seminary, where this is possible, and that the larger dioceses shall establish a minor seminary as well. Cf. II Plenary Council of Baltimore (1866), nn. 174, 175—*Coll. Lac.*, III, 449, c, d; 450, a; III Plenary Council of Baltimore (1884), n. 139. This plenary legislation requires at least one major seminary and one minor seminary in each province.

If, for example, there should be an undue number of mixed marriages in one or more of the dioceses of the province,[10] it seems clear that all the dioceses must join hands and take united measures to cope with the situation. If some serious moral abuse should arise, an instruction, an exhortation, a command, a warning, or perhaps a sanction, coming with the authority of all the bishops of the province, will summon the needed attention and obedience. Superstitious practices, extravagances of devotion, or any species of commercialism in sacred things should not pass unnoticed, but should be corrected.[11]

C. Settlement of Controversies

The phrase *"ad controversias componendas"* appears to be to some extent a relic of the former legislation which referred chiefly to the settlement of judicial controversies. While the judicial power of the council has never been expressly revoked, still it is a power whose exercise is scarcely practical today.[12] The provincial council ordinarily meets only at twenty year intervals,[13] convenes for just a few days, and lacks judicial competence over residential bishops[14] and over titular bishops, except in contentious cases.[15]

Augustine (1872-1943)[16] explained that the phrase "settling controversies" refers rather to the settling of questions arising in disciplinary matters, such as the administration of the Sacraments, the setting of parish boundaries, and the manner of education for the clergy and the faithful in seminaries and schools. Division and discord which become attendant upon conflicting practices relative to the celebration of mixed marriages or to the granting of matrimonial dispensations may be corrected through unifying provincial legislation. In a restricted sense, the Fathers of the council could settle

[10] Cf. canons 1060 and 1061.

[11] Fagnanus, Lib. V, tit. 1, cap. 25, n. 94.

[12] Wernz-Vidal, II, 682; De Meester, II, 116.

[13] Canon 283.

[14] Canon 1557. § 1. Cf. *infra*, p. 70, note 73, concerning the judicial exemptions of those who are regarded in law as equivalent to bishops.

[15] Canon 1557, § 2.

[16] *Commentary*, II, 305.

controversies, which had become dangerous to the interests of religion, by commanding silence, or by explaining the already defined doctrine of the Church.

D. Uniformity of Discipline

At the present day, with easy and rapid modes of transportation and with the constant flow of inter-city and inter-state business and social activities, the relationship between dioceses is closer and the need for uniform ecclesiastical discipline is especially felt. Chelodi (1880-1922) pointed out that under modern circumstances uniformity of discipline is of particular utility and corresponds to the aims of the current law.[17]

It may be observed that canon 290 lays special emphasis upon the need for "the preservation or establishment of *one and the same* discipline" (*"ad unam eandemque disciplinam servandam vel inducendam"*), in a manner not found in previous legislation. Wide discrepancy of discipline in a province weakens the administration of each diocese. Variations in adjacent dioceses in the observance of ecclesiastical laws, such as those of fasting and abstinence, can be a cause of bewilderment to the faithful. Scandal, carelessness, a lessened fidelity to the laws of the Church all too easily follow.[18]

Problems of government or discipline, which might appear too formidable for a bishop to meet single-handed, yield more readily to the united action taken by the bishops of an entire province after serious mutual deliberation. If variations in discipline and relaxations from the common law are not allowed to remain uncorrected, but are regulated uniformly, the government of each diocese will be facilitated and strengthened. Regulations for the granting of matrimonial dispensations, and ordinances expediting the proper perform-

[17] *Ius de Personis*, p. 392, note 4.

[18] Bishop John England (1786-1842), in a letter requesting the calling of a provincial council, wrote to his metropolitan archbishop (Maréchal, 1764-1828) on June 25, 1827: ". . . each Diocess [sic] is affected more or less by the disorder, or the other evils existing in any other . . ."—quoted from the Baltimore Cathedral Archives, Case 16, K 25 by Guilday, *The Life and Times of John England* (2 vols., New York: The America Press, 1927), II, 108.

ance of the duties of those who serve in diocesan curias or in posts of pastoral responsibility, the care of the Oriental Catholics, the promotion of divine worship, the setting of convenient hours in the public celebration of Mass for the faithful, the consistent practice of preaching, the devout administration of the Sacraments and the sacramentals, the generous support of seminaries, of hospitals, of schools, of charitable institutions, of missionary projects and enterprises, the due establishment of blessed cemeteries, the uniform application of the liturgical rules in the conduct of burial, and the employment of safe and orderly methods in the administration of Church property—these and similar matters that have inter-diocesan implications may commend themselves to mild and prudent provincial legislation.

Article 2. Particular Objects of Legislation Specified in the Code

The Code expressly assigns certain matters to be determined by provincial councils. The establishing of a just and uniform standard in certain financial matters is desirable in order to preclude the occasion of immoderate demands, of controversy and of scandal.[19] Councils can also promote sound discipline in a province through the opportune sharing of additional faculties with the vicars forane, and through a discreet intervention in the matter of the ecclesiastical prohibition of books.[20]

A. Regulations Concerning Financial Matters

1. Fees and Offerings

The regulation of fees for the concession of dispensations and of other favors (i.e., acts of voluntary jurisdiction), of fees for the execution of rescripts by the Holy See, and of the standard offerings

[19] Canon 1234, § 1, which refers to the establishing of a uniform standard of diocesan funeral fees by the bishop, suggests as the reason: . . . ita ut quaelibet contentionum et scandali removeatur occasio.

[20] Canons 447, § 1; 899, § 2; and 1395, § 1.

receivable on the occasion of the administration of the Sacraments and the sacramentals is an obligation incumbent on the bishops of a province. It rests within their option to fulfill this obligation either by means of a decree enacted in the provincial council, or by means of an ordinance formulated by them when convened in an extra-conciliar meeting in the province. But, the Holy See's approval is required for the valid determination of these fees and offerings.[21] The council cannot determine fees for the obtaining of matrimonial dispensations, since such fees are unlawful.[22] Nor has it the right to determine fees for funerals, since this right is assigned to the local ordinary.[23] A uniform standard of fees for ordinary judicial expenses is also to be established in the province through the medium of a provincial council or of a convention of the comprovincial bishops. The schedule of fees will include those which become payable to the diocesan curia for the expenses sustained by the tribunal in the judicial process; [24] it will also standardize the fees which become payable for the services of the advocates, the procurators, and for the

[21] Canon 1507, § 1.

[22] Canon 1056 forbids the exacting of a fee on the occasion of the granting of matrimonial dispensations, unless for the levying of such fee the express permission of the Holy See has been obtained. In reimbursement simply for the chancery expenses a moderate charge may be imposed, however, on such persons as are not financially straitened.

[23] Canon 1234, § 1. Canons 831, § 1, and 832 give the local ordinary the right to define both the maximum and the minimum amount that may be asked when the faithful contribute manual Mass stipends.

[24] Cf. canons 1909, § 1; 1507, § 2. Cf. Roberti, *De Processibus* (2 vols., Vol. I, 2. ed., 3. impressio, Romae: Apud Custodiam Librariam Pontificii Instituti Utriusque Iuris, 1941), I, 457. "Hodie iudices et tribunalis ministri nihil directe a partibus recipiunt . . . officialis, vice-officialis, promotor iustitiae, defensor vinculi, notarii, cursores, sua generatim habent certa stipendia a Curia diocesana. Iudices synodales saepius fere gratuitam operam praestant, et aliunde recipiunt sustentationem . . . Partes autem praeter expensas iudiciales quae aliis cedunt (testibus, peritis, etc.), certas taxas tribunali solvere tenentur . . . Hae omnes taxae Curiae aerarium ingrediuntur et indirecte inserviunt ad expensas tribunalium sustinendas." Cf. canon 1624; Wernz-Vidal, VI, 134; Beste, *Introductio in Codicem*, p. 778.

preparing and furnishing of judicial transcripts. The Code does not require that this schedule of fees be submitted for the Holy See's approval.[25]

The Sacred Congregation of the Council has stated that uniformity of taxes must prevail, not only in the diocese, but in the entire province. In other words, it is contrary to the law so to define taxes that only a maximum and minimum rate are set for the province, and it is left for the ordinaries in their respective diiceses to fix the rates within the designated limits. For by such an arrangement would be lost the uniformity which is the purpose of the law, and which if sacrificed would lead to wonderment and scandal on the part of the faithful.[26]

2. *Cathedraticum*

The *cathedraticum,* as described in canon 1504, is a moderate tax payable to the bishop annually as a sign of subjection to him and of honor to his episcopal office by all churches, benefices and lay confraternities of his jurisdiction.[27] It should be noted carefully that the *cathedraticum,* while subject to determination by either the provincial council or a conference of the comprovincial bishops, or also in accord with ancient custom,[28] is a tax which is to be uniform for all churches, benefices and lay confraternities of the province; it is to be in the nature of a tribute, and not a means of support for diocesan administration; it is to be a tax of very modest proportions, which does not prove burdensome to any single church, benefice or confraternity of the province.[29]

[25] Cf. canons 1909, § 1; 1507, § 2; Ayrinhac, *Administrative Legislation in the New Code of Canon Law* (New York: Longmans, Green, 1930), p. 407; Vermeersch-Creusen, *Epitome,* II, 577.

[26] S. C. C., 11 dec. 1920—*AAS,* XIII (1921), 350, 351.

[27] Exempt religious are not included in the obligation of paying the *cathedraticum,* unless a diocesan church, chapel or parish is entrusted to them. Confraternities of lay persons must pay the *cathedraticum* only if they have their own proper church. Simple pious associations which use the parish church are not subject to the tax. Cf. S. C. C., 13 mart. 1920—*AAS,* XII (1920), 445, 446; Augustine, *Commentary,* VI, 562, 563.

[28] Canon 1504.

[29] Augustine (*ibid.,* p. 563) estimates that the ancient *cathedraticum* approx-

"Ancient custom" as a legitimate determinant of the amount of the *cathedraticum* may be interpreted as a custom of forty years' duration.[30] Vermeersch-Creusen [31] rightly point out that the *cathedraticum* cannot be exacted unless it has been specified according to the norms of canon 1504. Although the bishop may freely waive the payment of the *cathedraticum,* his right to its payment is not subject to adverse prescription.[32] On the other hand, an individual bishop is not granted the competency to establish the amount of the *cathedraticum* for his diocese, since this practice would be counter to canon 1504. Moreover, since this canon specifies the bishop and not the local ordinary as the recipient of the tax, the *cathedraticum* is not subject to payment to the vicar capitular or diocesan administrator, *sede vacante.*[33]

The *dioecesanum,* not a uniform tribute, but an assessment proportioned to the size and revenue of each diocesan benefice, is intended to supply the support of diocesan administration, and hence must be sedulously distinguished from the *cathedraticum.*[34] The *dioecesanum* and the *cathedraticum* are not juridically convertible

imated six dollars. The Sacred Congregation of the Council (13 mart. 1920—*AAS,* XII [1920], 446) referred to the *cathedraticum* (which approximated ten francs or about two dollars) as established by the Council of Rome (1725) in order to illustrate the moderate and fixed nature of the *cathedraticum,* but the Sacred Congregation did not declare that it was establishing a restrictive maximum norm. Local circumstances and current money values are factors to be considered by the provincial council in its determination of the amount of the *cathedraticum,* which should, however, be fixed, and not vary from year to year.

[30] Coronata, *Inst.,* II, 447.

[31] *Epitome,* II, 575.

[32] Cf. canon 1509, 8°

[33] S. C. C., 20 aug. 1917—*AAS,* IX (1917), 500.

[34] Cf. Kremer, *Church Support in the United States,* The Catholic University of America Canon Law Studies, n. 61 (Washington, D. C.: The Catholic University of America, 1930), pp. 122, 123. Bouscaren-Ellis, *Canon Law, A Text and Commentary* (Milwaukee: Bruce, 1946), p. 742: ". . . it is evident that the use of the term *cathedraticum* to designate the tax levied by Bishops in the United States for the support of their dioceses is not accurate."

terms. Patently, the *dioecesanum* is not comprehended under canon 1504: the Code does not refer the determination of the *dioecesanum* to provincial councils.[85]

So far as the exaction of the *dioecesanum* has been tolerated, it has been the practical mind of the Holy See that it must be regulated for the individual diocese, and not made necessarily uniform for the province, since wide variations may exist in the financial circumstances of the dioceses within the same province.[86] Plenary law in the United States has placed the regulation of the *dioecesanum* within the competency, not of provincial councils, but of diocesan synods.[87]

[85] In the United States, where a *mensa episcopalis* is not had, the *dioecesanum* has been the established, customary means of support for diocesan administration. Although this practice is apparently an exception to the common law (as it was even before the Code), it has been a matter of practical necessity here, and may be regarded as having the recognition and at least tacit approbation of the Holy See. Cf. Kremer, *ibid.*, pp. 115-125; Beste, *Introductio in Codicem*, p. 728; Bouscaren-Ellis, *Canon Law, a Text and Commentary*, pp. 741-743; Ayrinhac, *Administrative Legislation in the New Code of Canon Law*, pp. 400-402; Wernz, III, n. 223. Cf. also the decree of the Sacred Congregation for the Oriental Church, on March 1, 1929 (for the Greek-Ruthenians in the United States), Article 7: "Annua *sustentatio* utriusque Episcopi consistet in praestationibus *ad instar cathedratici*, quae *iuxta aequitatem* ab Episcopo, audita voce suorum consultorum, determinabuntur, quasque singulae ecclesiae Ruthenorum Ordinariatuum solvere tenentur . . ." (italics by the writer)—*AAS*, XXI (1929), 154.

[86] The Sacred Congregation for the Propagation of the Faith, on February 16, 1857, in its Instruction concerning the decrees of the I Provincial Council of Cincinnati (1855), prescribed that the amount of the *dioecesanum* should be determined in diocesan synods rather than uniformly established for the entire province: "Amplitudo tua noscit agnitum fuisse jus Episcopi, ut ad sustinenda officii sui onera ex Dioecesi subsidia percipiat: applicatio tamen et determinatio subsidiorum opportunius fieri posse videtur in Synodis Dioecesanis, habita nimirum ratione ad uniuscujusque Dioeceseos statum et conditionem."—*Coll. Lac.*, III, 201, b. Cf. Kremer, *Church Support in the United States*, p. 121.

[87] II Plenary Council of Baltimore (1866), n. 100: "Demum, quum aequum plane sit ac justum, ut fideles omnes uniuscujusque Dioeceseos congruae contribuant sustentationi Episcopi, qui omnium gerit sollicitudinem, censuerunt Patres hac de re pertractandum in Dioecesanis Synodis, in quibus collatis inter

3. Salary of the Vicar Capitular and of the *Oeconomus*

The vicar capitular, as the administrator of a diocese, *sede vacante,* and the *oeconomus,* the financial administrator,[38] have a right to a just salary. The provincial council should determine the amount of the salaries of the vicar capitular and of the *oeconomus,* unless the matter has already been settled by the received custom of the province or by other legitimate provision governing the particular territory.[39]

se consiliis sacerdotes curam habentes animarum conveniant de certa pensione Ordinario quotannis tribuenda, quae ex portione singularum ecclesiarum reddituum [sic] determinata coalescat. Ejusmodi autem adsignatio vel distributio, cum fuerit ab Ordinario recognita ac probata, ceu lex Dioecesana ab omnibus servanda evulgabitur."—*Coll. Lac.,* III, 429, b.

The provision that the *dioecesanum* must not be established in excess of 10% of the parochial revenues (cf. VIII Provincial Council of Baltimore [1855], n. 7—*Coll. Lac.,* III, 162, b, c) is still in effect as plenary law for the United States, since the II Plenary Council of Baltimore (1866) incorporated all legislation of the preceding Councils of Baltimore. Cf. II Plenary Council of Baltimore (1866), n. 533—*Coll. Lac.,* III, 544, b.

Worthy of commendation in the writer's opinion, is the legislation of the IV Provincial Council of Portland (1932), which determined the amount of the salaries of the metropolitan and the bishops, and explained the nature of the *dioecesanum,* but observed the right of the diocesan synods to regulate the amount of the *dioecesanum,* the general diocesan fund, from which the bishop's salary is but one item of expenditure. Cf. IV Provincial Council of Portland (1932), nn. 366, 368, 369—*Acta et Decreta Concilii Provincialis Portlandensis in Oregon Quarti, Portlandiae in Ecclesia Metropolitana Celebrati, Diebus,* VIII, IX, X *Septembris MCMXXXII* (Portland: The Sentinel Printery, 1934), pp. 127, 128.

[38] Cf. Coronata, *Inst.,* I, 540: "Constituendus est oeconomus in dioecesibus ubi ad Capitulum, sede vacante, praeter dioecesis regimen, etiam ius fructuum mensae episcopalis percipiendorum incumbit." Cf. Coronata, *ibid.,* note 1: ". . . Unde si fructus percipiendi aut nulli sunt, aut alio modo iam provisum est, oeconomi constitutio inutilis evadit. Id etiam ante Codicem ob defectum conditionis accidebat . . ." Cf. canon 433, § 3; Jaeger, *The Administration of Vacant and Quasi-Vacant Episcopal Sees in the United States,* The Catholic University of America Canon Law Studies, n. 81 (Washington, D. C.: The Catholic University of America, 1932), pp. 108-109.

[39] Canon 441, § 1.

B. Faculties of the Vicar Forane

The office of the vicar forane (or rural dean) is given special attention by the law in the matter of specifying his faculties. The Code not only enumerates the rights and duties of the vicar forane, but canon 447, § 1, makes mention of the fact that he may possess additional faculties by virtue of the bishop's concession or through a synodal or provincial decree. The dean's faculties should be wisely moderated; if they are too rigidly restricted or too loosely defined, the good of souls may suffer. For the sake of a uniform pastoral discipline, provincial councils can specify certain faculties and duties for vicars forane, and these faculties and duties, unless the law stated otherwise, could be supplemented at the will of the bishop.[40]

C. Prohibition of Books

The office of safeguarding the faithful from the baneful influences of obscene and irreligious books, by their prohibition, is assigned not only to ordinaries for their dioceses but to provincial councils for the protection of the entire province.[41] In each diocese a "Council of Vigilance," as ordered by Pope Pius X,[42] should be instituted in order to detect evil books and to secure their prohibition.

[40] Zaplotnik, *De Vicariis Foraneis,* The Catholic University of America Canon Law Studies, n. 47 (Washington, D. C.: The Catholic University of America, 1927), pp. 80, 81: "Objectum facultatum Vicario foraneo concedendarum debet esse materia quae non excedit competentiam Episcopi, e. gr. absolutio a censuris et peccatis Episcopo reservatis, dispensatio a lege aliqua dioecesana, ab impedimentis matrimonialibus, irregularitatibus, votis privatis; potestas dandi licentam binandi, concionandi, discedendi a paroecia pro parochis eorumque vicariis, peragendi varias solemnes benedictiones, invigilandi instructioni iuventutis in scholis, introducendi parochos novos in eorum paroecias, corrigendi varios abusus." Cf. Wernz-Vidal, II, 909.

[41] Canon 1395, § 1: Ius et officium libros ex iusta causa prohibendi competit non solum supremae auctoritati ecclesiasticae pro universa Ecclesia, sed pro suis subditis Conciliis quoque particularibus et locorum Ordinariis.

[42] Litt. encycl. *"Pascendi,"* 8 sept. 1907, n. 44—*Fontes,* n. 680. The prescription regarding the establishment of diocesan "Councils of Vigilance" since it was decreed only as a temporary measure against current modernistic errors was not included in the stable legislation of the Code. However, the prescription for the diocesan "Councils of Vigilance" is to continue in force until the Holy

The prohibition of books is an act of ecclesiastical jurisdiction whereby the faithful are forbidden to read certain specified immoral or harmful books.[43] Such prohibition extends to the publishing, reading, retaining, selling, translating or communicating of the books to others in any manner.[44]

The evil of bad books readily seeps from city to city, and from a single diocese it can spread throughout the province. Hence there is a need for vigilance, common counsel and united action, which can efficiently be provided by a provincial council.

Recourse against the provincial council's prohibition of books may be made to Rome, but such a recourse is not endowed with any suspensive effect relative to what was commanded to be observed. The decreed prohibition of books must be obeyed until the Holy See has ruled otherwise.[45]

Article 3. Methods of Legislation

A. Antecedent Deliberation

The value of provincial laws is considerably enhanced because of the fact that they are the result of serious deliberation and of common counsel. What Hanrahan says of plenary councils may be applied equally well here:

> Another feature of plenary councils which accounts for the Church's favorable attitude towards them is the fact that the laws enacted are the result of consultation and discussion. To hear the opinions of others, to become conversant with the pros and cons before taking action, is to imitate the Popes themselves.[46]

The first step in the framing of provincial laws is provided for in canon 292. This canon requires that at least every five years the

See rules otherwise. Cf. S. C. S. Off., decr. (circa concilia a vigilantia et iuramentum antimodernisticum), 22 mart. 1918—*AAS,* X (1918), 136; Bouscaren, I, 50, 51.

[43] Wernz-Vidal, IV, pars. II, 153.

[44] Canon 1398, § 1; Vermeersch-Creusen, *Epitome,* II, 512.

[45] Canon 1395, § 2.

[46] "The Law on Plenary Councils"—*The Clergy Review,* XIV (1938), 391.

bishops of the province convene and prepare matters to be treated at the next council. A practice has developed of imitating the method used in the formulating of our present Code, by appointing, well in advance of the council, commissions of canonists and theologians, to analyze and coordinate specific points of proposed legislation.[47] This procedure is not directed by law, as it is in the case of the diocesan synod,[48] but is very useful and may be employed with the consent of the bishops. The metropolitan must be guided by the will of the majority in these details, since it is not a point left to his discretion by the law, and since the rights of all the prelates are equally involved.[49] Also useful, if it so pleases the Fathers, is the calling of sessions preparatory to the council.[50]

B. Modes of Legislation

1. Laws *Secundum Ius* and *Praeter Ius*

The model for the provincial council's legislative activity is the Code of Canon Law. The closer the council cleaves to the spirit of the Code, the more exactly the council secures the uniform observance of the common law, the happier will be the outcome. The council may, without conflict with the law, enact measures which are *secundum ius commune*, or *praeter ius commune*.[51] But the

[47] Hanrahan, "art. cit."—*The Clergy Review*, XIV (1938), 399.

[48] Canon 360, § 1, directs the bishop to appoint preliminary commissions to prepare matters to be treated in the diocesan synod, if he judges it expedient.

[49] Cf. canons 288; 289; 292. In these canons the equality of all the bishops in arriving at decisions is indicated.

[50] At the IV Provincial Council of Portland, Oregon, which was celebrated September 8-10, 1932, four preparatory sessions, attended by the bishops and (in the later sessions) by canonists and theologians also, were held at intervals of about three months. Cf. *Acta et Decreta Concilii Provincialis Portlandensis in Oregon Quarti* (1932), pp. 15-20.

[51] Conciliar decrees which are *contra ius commune* are *ipso facto* invalid. But a provincial council is an apt occasion for requesting an indult from the Holy See, if particular conditions in the province render excessively difficult the observance of some phase of the common law. Fagnanus (Lib. V, tit. 1, cap. 25, n. 95) suggested that the prelates send an appendix of proposals to the Holy Father concerning means of securing the progress of the province in ecclesiastical discipline and of meeting difficulties, obstacles and perils.

latter class of laws, which concern matters not contained in the Code, should be used sparingly. If too many laws *praeter ius* are enacted, the authority of the individual bishops is unduly hampered and their free jurisdiction is absorbed, as it were, in a manner which is not intended by the law.[52] Since the time of the IV Council of the Lateran (1215), special emphasis has been laid upon the office of the provincial councils in executing the general laws of the Church.[53] The universal laws of the Church must be published in such a way that they will be well known and will be brought to practical application in the province. When some portion of the law is not being observed, when ecclesiastical matters in the province need correction, the provincial council acts as the auxiliary of the common law by enacting corrective measures.[54]

2. Corrective Measures

a. Milder Forms

How is this correction to be made? A mere repetition of the laws of the Code is not generally to be recommended, although an arrangement of the decrees according to the order of the canons of the Code and with references to the Code appears to be very practical.[55] Such an arrangement will favor brevity in the decrees, which is of great advantage. Excessive legislation is a form of over-emphasis, which weakens the force of the body of laws. And the multiplying of laws may pave the way for measures which will prove to be harmful rather than helpful. In this, as in other important matters, it is better to make haste slowly.[56]

[52] Wernz, I, n. 181.

[53] C. 25, X, *de accusationibus, inquisitionibus et denunciationibus*, V, 1; Gousset, p. 274.

[54] Cf. *supra*, p. 20, note 119.

[55] Cf. Donnelly, *The Diocesan Synod*, p. 88.

[56] Cf. letter of Bishop England to Archbishop Whitfield (1770-1834), December 26, 1828: "I think our decisions at first should be made as few as possible, for it is easier to supply at a future period what might be wanting than to retract what would have been once done."—quoted from the Baltimore Cathedral Archives, Case 23, G 2, by Guilday, *The Life and Times of John England*, II, 117.

Both innovations of law and excessive rigor should be avoided by provincial councils.[57] The Church favors mildness rather than severity in her laws, and in a canon which is strikingly different from all others in that it contains a lengthy quotation the Code stresses the fact that benevolence often avails more than severity.[58] Bishops are urged to pursue their office in the spirit of fatherly love, and with exhortation and warning to deter their subjects from errors which would necessitate the invoking of penalties. When mistakes occur through human frailty, bishops should correct them kindly and patiently, but errors should not be allowed to escape unheeded until they grow in strength and become deeply rooted.

Fagnanus (1598-1678), who was for many years secretary of the Sacred Congregation of the Council and therefore in a position to make close observations, advised that the council should promote the more exact and ready observance of the common law through the medium of particular regulations and that, with due regard and adaptation to the persons and matters involved, the Fathers should now teach, now exhort, and now threaten. He also mentioned that upon delinquents the Council was to inflict the penalties for which these persons were liable.[59]

b. Penalties

Penalties should be employed only as a last resort. But since provincial councils must execute the laws of the Church, the Fathers

[57] Chelodi, *Ius de Personis,* p. 392, note 4.

[58] Canon 2214, § 2, quotes from the Council of Trent, sess. XIII, *de ref.*, c. 1.

[59] *Commentaria in Quinque Decretalium Libros,* Lib. V, tit. 1, cap. 25, n. 13: "Conveniebant olim in unum Episcopi ut de incidentibus casibus fieret disceptatio, et salubris de Ecclesiastica observatione collatio, quatenus et praeterita corrigerentur, et regulam futura susciperent . . . Haec autem fere praestabantur, canonicas regulas, maxime quae in ultimo generali Concilio statutae essent, relegendo; debitas poenas transgressoribus infligendo . . . nonnulla etiam ad majorem facilioremque observationem sacrorum Canonum per modum regulae dirigendo, ac prout rerum, et personarum qualitates, postulant, erudiendo, comminando, et exhortando . . ."

are obliged to invoke sanctions [60] when they are necessary to secure the observance of the law. The vindicative penalties,[61] penal remedies [62] and penances [63] may be employed within the limits prescribed by the common law.[64]

But the coactive power of provincial councils is restricted in regard to the following classes of persons:

> (1) those who hold the highest governmental rank in a nation or state, their children, and their proximate successors in office;
> (2) cardinals;
> (3) legates of the Holy See; and
> (4) bishops, whether residential or titular.

The reason for this limitation is that these persons cannot be punished by anyone less than the Holy Father, as stated in canon 2227, § 1.[65]

Some conflict appears between canon 2220, § 1 (which gives coactive power to the legislator, in this case the council, over those subject to the law, including the above mentioned persons), and canon 2227, § 1. Canon 2227, § 2, refers to *latae sententiae* penalties of the common law. From the context, could the terms of canon 2227, § 1, be restricted to *ferendae sententiae* penalties, as the word "*infligi*" suggests,[66] and to declaratory sentences of *latae sententiae* penalties, as the word "*declarari*" suggests? [67] If so, the council would have the power to join *latae sententiae* penalties to its laws, and the persons privileged in canon 1557, § 1, would be subject to

[60] Provincial councils have ordinary coactive power. Cf. canon 2220, § 1: Qui pollent potestate leges ferendi vel praecepta imponendi, possunt quoque legi vel praecepto poenas adnectere . . .; cf. Wernz-Vidal, II, 681.

[61] Canons 2291; 2298.

[62] Canon 2306.

[63] Canon 2313.

[64] Thus deposition, for instance, is restricted to the cases expressed in the Code; cf. canon 2303, § 3.

[65] Canon 2227, § 1: Poena nonnisi a Romano Pontifice infligi aut declarari potest in eos de quibus in can. 1557, § 1.

[66] Cf. canon 2217, § 1, 2°: . . . *ferendae sententiae,* si a iudice vel Superiore *infligi* [italics by the writer] debeat.

[67] Cf. canon 2225: Si poena *declaretur vel infligatur* per sententiam iudicialem . . . (Italics are the writer's.)

these penalties. However, in penalties the benign interpretation is to be made.[68] The milder interpretation requires that the word "*infligi*" of canon 2227, § 1, which is not expressly and definitely restricted to *ferendae sententiae* penalties, should be taken in a general sense, extending also to *latae sententiae* penalties. Therefore the view of Vermeersch-Creusn,[69] Coronata,[70] Blat [71] and Chelodi [72] appears to be sustained, namely, that bishops and the other privileged persons mentioned in canon 1557, § 1, are not subject to penalties enacted by anyone inferior to the Roman Pontiff. They are therefore exempt from the penalties invoked by provincial councils.[73]

[68] Canon 2219, § 1.

[69] *Epitome*, III, 247: "[Personae relatae in canone 1557, § 1] non subduntur poenis quae legibus particularibus adduntur."

[70] Explaining canon 2227, § 2, Coronata (*Inst.*, IV, 109) states: "Agitur hic de poenis lege universali seu pontificia contentis; nam legibus particularibus nisi a R. Pontifice *specialiter* approbatae fuerint, ne comprehendi quidem expresse possunt Episcopi etiam titulares et S. R. E. Cardinales, necnon Apostolicae Sedis Legati."

[71] *Commentarium*, VI, 70.

[72] *Ius Poenale et Ordo Procedendi in Iudiciis Criminalibus iuxta Codicem Iuris Canonici* (Tridenti: Libr. Edit. Tridentium, 1925), pp. 28, 29. Chelodi states that bishops are subject to [penal] laws and penal sentences of the Roman Pontiff alone.

[73] Abbots and prelates *nullius* (cf. canons 215, § 2, and 323, § 1), vicars and prefects apostolic (cf. canon 294, § 1) and permanent apostolic administrators (cf. canon 315, § 1) are placed by the law on an equal juridical basis with bishops, and hence seem to enjoy the judicial and penal exemptions accorded by canons 1557, § 1, and 2227, § 1. Coronata (*Inst.*, III, p. 11, note 7) supports this opinion, at least so far as abbots and prelates *nullius* are concerned; cf. also Coronata, *ibid.*, note 8. Cf. Cavigioli, *De Censuris Latae Sententiae Quae in Codice Juris Canonici Continentur Commentariolum* (Torino, 1919), nn. 11, 23.

The opposite opinion is held by Roberti (*De Processibus*, I, 184): "Haec reservatio canonis 1557, § 1, 3°, videtur inniti in charactere episcopali; quare non extenditur ad rectores diocesium qui hoc charactere carent." But the view of Roberti implies that the word *Episcopos* is used in different senses in canons 1557, § 1, 3°, and 1557, § 2, 1°, whereas, more correctly, it seems that not the words *Episcopos* but rather *titulares* and *residentiales* are in contradistinction in these references, and it apparently removes the distinction between *in criminalibus* (1557, § 1, 3°) and *in contentiosis* (1557, § 2, 1°), for the author

The censures of excommunication, suspension and interdict may be employed also, but only with great caution and circumspection,[74] and only against delicts which are external, grave, completely executed and committed contumaciously.[75] For the reservation of censures there is the further restriction that such action be required because of the particular gravity of the offenses and the necessity of more effectively safeguarding ecclesiastical discipline and public morals.[76]

c. *Reservation of Sins*

The power to reserve sins to each of the ordinaries uniformly throughout the province also belongs to the provincial council,[77] since the council has ordinary power of jurisdiction, including the power to inflict censures.[78] However, the writer is of the opinion that the conditions prescribed for the reservation of sins [79] dissuade the use of this power except under extreme circumstances and with generous concessions to the dispensing power of the ordinaries. For

(*ibid.*, p. 185) in his commentary on canon 1557, § 2, 1°, adds: ". . . Episcopis aequiparandi sunt Abbates et Praelati nullius (c. 215, § 2), nec non Vicarii et Praefecti Apostolici (c. 294, § 1) itemque, uti videtur, Administratores Apostolici, Vicarii Capitulares nec non omnes qui praesunt regimini dioecesium. Hi, si charactere episcopali careant, etiam quoad causas *criminales* tribunalibus S. Sedis subiciuntur." If Roberti is correct in stating (*loc. cit.*) that all local ordinaries, except vicars general, must in the present instance be regarded as equivalent to (residential) bishops, it seems that they should be included under canon 1557, § 1, 3°, as well as under canon 1557, § 2, 1°.

[74] Canon 2241, § 2.

[75] Canon 2242, § 1.

[76] Canon 2246, § 1.

[77] Cf. Benedictus XIV, *De Syn.*, Lib. V, cap. 4, n. 3; Nevin, "Power of Plenary Council to Reserve Sins"—*The Australasian Catholic Record,* VIII (1931), 228-231.

[78] Cf. canon 893, § 1.

[79] Canon 897: Casus reservandi sint pauci omnino, tres scilicet vel, ad summum, quatuor ex gravioribus tantum et atrocioribus criminibus externis specifice determinatis; ipsa vero reservatio ne ultra in vigore maneat, quam necesse sit ad publicum aliquod inolitum vitium exstirpandum et collapsam forte christianam disciplinam instaurandam.

the reservation of sins should remain in force only so long as it is necessary for the extirpation of a deeply entrenched and public vice, whereas, unless otherwise qualified, the reservation of sins by provincial councils would ordinarily continue for twenty years, since this is legally the maximum interval between councils.[80]

[80] Canon 283.

CHAPTER V

CONVOCATION OF THE PROVINCIAL COUNCIL

ARTICLE 1. RIGHT AND OBLIGATION TO CONVOKE THE COUNCIL

A. Of the Metropolitan

Canon 284. Metropolita . . .
2°. Concilium convocat eique praeest.

The ancient rule which conferred upon the metropolitan the rights of convoking and of presiding at the council [1] is still retained in the present law. The office of notifying the suffragan bishops and other members, and of calling them to the provincial council, is exclusively the right and obligation of the metropolitan, unless he is legitimately impeded.[2]

It is only after the reception of the *pallium* that the metropolitan can licitly convoke and celebrate a council,[3] and hence only a metropolitan understood in the strict sense of the word has the right and obligation in question.[4] For this reason, and from concordant testimony of the authors, convocation is to be made by the metropolitan

[1] Can. 20, Council of Antioch (341)—Bruns, I, 85, 86; can. 16, Council of Antioch (341)—Bruns, I, 85; can. 6, IV Council of the Lateran (1215)—Mansi, XXII, 991; c. 25, X, *de accusationibus, inquisitionibus et denunciationibus,* V, 1; Conc. Trident., sess. XXIV, *de ref.,* c. 2.

[2] Conc. Trident., sess. XXIV, *de ref.,* c. 2; cf. *infra,* in the present Chapter, Article 2, concerning the law of convocation in places subject to the Sacred Congregation for the Propagation of the Faith, as provided for in canon 304, § 2.

[3] Cf. canon 276, which admits only a special apostolic indult by way of exception; cf. also *Pontificale Romanum,* tit. *De pallio,* § V; c. 28, X, *de electione,* I, 6; Beste, *Introductio in Codicem,* p. 253; Wernz-Vidal, II, 677; Toso, *Commentaria Minora,* III, 101.

[4] Wernz-Vidal, *loc. cit.*; S. C. C., *Tarraconen.,* 10 febr. 1624—*Fontes,* n. 2448; Benedictus XIV, *De Syn.,* Lib. II, cap. 9, n. 8. Canon 284 makes it clear that when the metropolitan see is vacant neither the vicar capitular nor the cathedral chapter have the right of convoking the council.

personally and not through his vicar general, since even with a special mandate from the metropolitan, a convocation made by the vicar general would be null.[5] So essential is this right and office of the metropolitan that without a legitimate convocation a provincial council would lack all juridical force.[6]

In choosing the time for the celebration of the council the metropolitan should be guided by the directions of the liturgical books [7]

[5] Authors agree that a convocation through the vicar general would be null, from the literal meaning of the Tridentine decree (sess. XXIV, *de ref.*, c. 2): "Metropolitani *per seipsos* [emphasis added], seu illis legitime impeditis, coepiscopus antiquior . . . non praetermittant synodum in provincia sua cogere . . ."; cf. Petra, *Commentaria*, I, p. 277, n. 19; Bouix, *De Concilio Provinciali*, p. 101; Coronata, *Compendium Iuris Canonici* (2 vols., Taurini: Marietti, 1937-1938), I, 375.

Similarly, the coadjutor or auxiliary bishop to the metropolitan cannot validly convoke provincial councils. A coadjutor bishop who possesses full powers of diocesan administration together with the right of succession to the metropolitan see becomes the principal bishop of the archdiocese and obtains the metropolitan office only at the moment of the see's vacancy. Cf. canons 355, § 1; 430, §§ 1, 3; Lynch, *Coadjutors and Auxiliaries of Bishops*, The Catholic University of America Canon Law Studies, n. 238 (Washington, D. C.: The Catholic University of America Press, 1947), pp. 83, 84.

[6] Petra, *ibid.*, n. 18; Toso, *Commentaria Minora*, III, 109.

[7] Cf. *Caeremoniale Episcoporum*, Lib. I, cap. 31, n. 3: "Primo erit advertendum, praesertim in Concilio Provinciali habendo, ut dies inchoationis hujusmodi Concilii per publica documenta omnibus, qui de jure, vel consuetudine interesse debent, denuntietur . . ." For examples of edicts and letters of convocation, cf. *Coll. Lac.*, VI, 1; 2; 127, c, d; 128, a, b, c; 134, b, c; 135, a, b; 286, b, c, d; 427; 428; 452-455, a; 562, c; 563, a. The *Caeremoniale Episcoporum* (*ibid.*, nn. 3, 4) suggests that besides the required formal convocation, for the sake of wider publicity, announcement of the forthcoming council can be made in the cathedral churches (and laudably also in the parish churches) at Mass on the feast of the Epiphany. Also, during the two months, or at least within the month, preceding the council, the edict of convocation can be affixed to the doors of all churches of prelates who enjoy a deliberative conciliar vote. On the three Sundays before the council it will be appropriate to announce the approaching council from the pulpits of all cathedral and parish churches, and to exhort the faithful to prayer, fasting, the reception of the Sacraments and the performance of pious works, in order to secure God's blessing upon the council. "It is usual on such occasions that the Bishop of each Diocese order the Collect *De Spiritu Sancto*, to be added at Mass every day till the conclusion of the Council."—*Ceremonial for the Use of the Catholic Churches in*

and the demands of reason and justice. Hence he could not ordinarily set the date of the council for a time when the law requires the presence of the bishops in their own cathedral church, namely, during the seasons of Advent and Lent, or on the feasts of Easter, Pentecost and Corpus Christi.[8]

Since the celebration of provincial councils is dependent upon their legitimate convocation, the obligation, as imposed by canon 283, of convoking a provincial council at least every twentieth year is personally incumbent upon the metropolitan. Formerly, this obligation was enforced with specific penal sanctions.[9] The penalties as formerly specified have not, however, been incorporated in the law of the present Code.[10]

B. Of the SUFFRAGANEUS ANTIQUIOR

The phase of the law which extends the right of convocation to the senior suffragan bishop of the province when the metropolitan is legitimately impeded, or when the metropolitan see is vacant, was introduced by the Council of Trent.[11] The senior suffragan bishop

the United States of America (8. ed. revised, Philadelphia, 1894), p. 377 (hereafter cited as *Baltimore Ceremonial*). Cf. Moretti (*Caeremoniale iuxta Ritum Romanum seu de Sacris Functionibus Episcopo Celebrante, Assistente, Absente* [4 vols., Taurini: Marietti, 1936-1939], III, nn. 2452, 2370, 1590, 1591 [hereafter cited as Moretti]), who seems, however, open to misunderstanding, since one might draw from the author the mistaken inference that not only the prescribed convocation but also the accompanying suggested directions of the *Caeremoniale Episcoporum* (as noted above) are strictly preceptive.

[8] Canon 338, § 3. The canon admits of exception in the case of a grave and urgent cause, but it is difficult to envision circumstances under which the celebration of the council could not be deferred for a short period, such as the Lenten season.

[9] Cf. *supra,* Chapter I, Article 1, B, 2.

[10] Cf. canon 6, 5°.

[11] Sess. XXIV, *de ref.,* c. 2. The Code adds the phrase *"vel sede archiepiscopali vacante,"* which was not stated explicitly in the Tridentine law. Cf. S. C. C., *Tarraconen.,* 10 febr. 1624—*Fontes,* n. 2448.

The vacancy of an episcopal see may occur in any of the following ways: through the death of the incumbent of the see, through his resignation, deprivation or removal from office, or in consequence of his transfer to another diocese. (Cf. canons 430, §§ 1, 3; 183, § 1.)

is that residential bishop who was first promoted to a diocesan see within the province.[12] An exempt prelate, as described in canon 285,[13] is not a suffragan bishop, and therefore cannot convoke a provincial council.[14]

Under the former law, Gousset (1792-1866)[15] maintained that the senior suffragan bishop was obliged to supply not only for a metropolitan who was legitimately impeded but also for one who was culpably neglectful. In support of his opinion he claimed that the law of holding councils obliged suffragans as much as it obliged the metropolitan.[16] But both the former and the present law seem clear on the point that the senior suffragan has only a devolved right and obligation, which does not exist unless two conditions are veri-

[12] Seniority in this matter is not determined according to the general norms of precedence, as stated in canon 106, 3°, since it is not measured from the time of episcopal consecration. Blat (*Commentarium,* II, 254) seems to hold that seniority for the developed obligation of convoking the council is determined from the time of establishment of the suffragan see, rather than from the time of the bishop's promotion to a suffragan see, but this opinion does not appear to be tenable.

[13] Bishops who are not subject to any metropolitan, or also abbots and prelates *nullius* and archbishops who have no suffragans, are termed exempt prelates or exempt bishops, because they are exempt from dependence upon a metropolitan and are immediately subject to the Holy See. They are required by canon 285 to select a neighboring metropolitan, with the Holy See's approval, and thereafter to participate in his provincial councils. Pre-Code legislation on this point did not mention either archbishops or abbots and prelates *nullius.* (Cf. *infra,* pp. 95, 96).

[14] Cf. Petra, *Commentaria,* I, p. 278, n. 31, where he cited a resolution of the Sacred Congregation of the Council of April 17, 1649 (not contained in the *Fontes* or in the *Collect.*); cf. *ibid.*, p. 277, n. 21; Fagnanus, Lib. V, tit. 1, cap. 25, n. 18; Bouix, *De Concilio Provinciali,* p. 98; Gousset, p. 261.

[15] *Exposition des Principes du Droit Canonique,* p. 262.

[16] The Tridentine law appeared to stress the obligation of the *suffraganeus antiquior* more than does the present law, for it commanded that the senior suffragan bishop should not omit to call the council when the metropolitan was legitimately impeded. Cf. sess. XXIV, *de ref.*, c. 2: "Metropolitani per seipsos, seu illis legitime impeditis, coepiscopus antiquior . . . *non praetermittat* Synodum in provincia sua cogere . . ." (Italics are the writer's.)

fied: first, that the metropolitan is *impeded,* and, secondly, that he is *legitimately* impeded.[17]

But when may it be said that the metropolitan is legitimately impeded? It seems to the writer that, in order to obviate the danger of controversies, the judge in this matter must ordinarily be the metropolitan himself. If, therefore, a grave reason, such as sickness or advanced age, would prevent the metropolitan from exercising the office, he should request the senior suffragan bishop to accept the responsibility for convoking and presiding at the council. Toso suggests, as an example of a legitimate impediment, the metropolitan's absence from the province, because of his occupation with a special office committed to him by the Holy Father.[18]

But at times it will not be possible for the senior suffragan bishop to consult with the metropolitan. Indeed, there are some cases enumerated in law as impeding the administration of a see, upon the very condition that it is impossible for the bishop to communicate with his subjects. The impediments described in this connection in canon 429, § 1,[19] seem applicable here. The canon under consideration mentions the captivity, exile, banishment or complete incapacity of a bishop as sufficient to effect the temporary transfer of the administration of the see, if the circumstances are such that the bishop cannot communicate even by letter with his subjects. The circumstance of a bishop's complete incapacity is verified only when his mental faculties fail to such an extent that he is incapable of a human act.[20] Since these circumstances are contemplated by

[17] Canon 284: "Metropolita, eoque *legitime* impedito vel sede archiepiscopali vacante, Suffraganeus antiquior . . . concilium convocat . . ." (Emphasis added.)

[18] *Commentaria Minora,* III, 106. The fact that the metropolitan had not yet received the *pallium* would constitute a legitimate impediment to his convoking or presiding over a council (cf. canon 276). However, the impediment of not having received the *pallium* would in practice be of rare occurrence, since the metropolitan is obliged to seek the *pallium* within three months from the time of his episcopal consecration or of his canonical appointment made in the Consistory. (Cf. canon 275.)

[19] Cf. Jaeger, *The Administration of Vacant and Quasi-Vacant Episcopal Sees in the United States,* pp. 213, 214.

[20] Jaeger, *ibid.,* p. 214; Wernz-Vidal, II, 896.

the law as grave enough to effect the transfer, for a time, of the administration of a see, it appears that they would establish adequately the fact that a metropolitan is legitimately impeded.[21]

It may be difficult to judge the existence of the metropolitan's incapacity in a concrete case. Recognition by the Holy See of the existence of such an impediment might occur, as in the sending of a coadjutor with full powers of administration to the metropolitan.[22] If one of the foregoing impediments is present, or the archiepiscopal see is vacant, the senior suffragan is empowered to convoke the council without further permission from the Holy See, and it becomes in fact his obligation to do so.[23] But if any doubt might be raised as to whether the metropolitan is legitimately impeded and if the question could not be settled by means of communicating with him, then the senior suffragan should confirm his right of convocation by securing the affirmative judgment of the Holy See.[24]

Is there any obligation for the senior suffragan bishop to notify the Holy See if the metropolitan fails in his duty to convoke the council? It does not appear so, since this obligation is not stated in the law.[25]

[21] Cf. Toso, *loc. cit.*, where these causes are cited.

[22] As noted above, the coadjutor bishop cannot claim the title of metropolitan and hence lacks the power to convoke or celebrate a provincial council (cf. *supra*, p. 74, note 5). Canon 275 indicates that the metropolitan must possess the *pallium* in order to convoke a council licitly. Apart from an apostolic privilege, the right to obtain and to use the *pallium* is strictly personal to the metropolitan alone. Cf. canons 275; 278; 279.

[23] Petra (*Commentaria*, I, p. 277, n. 22) stated that it was not necessary for the senior suffragan to obtain permission from the patriarch or the primate for the convoking of the council when the metropolitan was impeded or the see was vacant.

[24] Cf. Petra (*ibid.*, pp. 276, 277, nn. 12, 13), who advised that in addition to the required consent of the suffragans the metropolitan should notify the Sacred Congregation of the Council when he desired to call a council oftener than the law requires. Cardinal Petra (1662-1747) gave this advice in order to forestall all possible controversies between the metropolitan and the suffragan bishops.

[25] Toso (*Commentaria Minora*, III, 106) appears to hold the opposite opinion: "Quod si Metropolitae impedimentum legitimum non appareat, videtur

If the metropolitan should be illegitimately absent, he could not be said to be thereby legitimately impeded. In that case, therefore, the senior suffragan bishop would have the obligation of notifying the Holy See of the illegitimate absence (if it had lasted over six months),[26] but not of supplying personally for the metropolitan's reprehensible failure to convoke the council.

Article 2. Frequency of Convocation

Canon 283. In singulis provinciis ecclesiasticis celebretur provinciale Concilium vicesimo saltem quoque anno.

A. Vicesimo . . . Quoque Anno

In each ecclesiastical province a provincial council is to be celebrated at least every twenty years. It is a law which is stated without qualifications or exceptions.[27] But an exception to canon 283 apparently occurs in canon 304, § 2, which provides special regulations for mission territories which are subject to the Sacred Congregation for the Propagation of the Faith. For it is stated that in those regions there is no determined time for the celebration of councils.

Canon 304, § 2, has occasioned considerable difficulty for commentators. Wernz-Vidal [28] pointed out that in some mission places

oportere, ut Suffraganeus antiquior recursum interponat apud Ap. Sedem." Toso seems to refer not merely to cases of doubt, but also to cases in which it is evident that the metropolitan is not legitimately impeded.

[26] Canon 338, § 4: Si ultra sex menses e dioecesi illegitime abfuerint . . . Metropolitam antiquior Suffraganeus residens Sedi Apostolicae denuntiet.

[27] Exceptions can occur, of course, through particular laws of the Holy See. By decree of the Sacred Consistorial Congregation, plenary councils, instead of provincial councils, are to be held every twenty years in certain regions of Italy. The reason for this decree, which did not retract the prescriptions of canons 285 and 1594, was that in the specified regions of Italy the provinces are small, and not a few of them lack suffragan sees. Cf. S. C. Consist., 15 febr. 1919—*AAS,* XI (1919), 72-74; S. C. Consist., 22 mart. 1919 —*AAS,* XI (1919), 175-177; Sartori, *Enchiridion Canonicum,* pp. 29, 30; Coronata, *Inst.,* I, p. 422, note 5.

[28] *Ius Canonicum,* II, 696.

which are subject to the Sacred Congregation for the Propagation of the Faith there coexist both vicariates and prefectures apostolic and some regularly erected dioceses, together with an archdiocese. Their inference was that it is only to such places where an ecclesiastical province has been already constituted that canon 304, § 2, refers.[29] Moreover, the permission of the Holy See is required for the convocation of such councils, according to the same authors.

Sipos [30] holds that councils can be celebrated only in those mission places where residential bishops have been established. Coronata [31] with some hesitation accedes to the explanation of Wernz-Vidal. Chelodi,[32] however, understood canon 304 as contemplating mission places which were unattached to provinces and lacked the authority of metropolitans. In support of his view it may be said that the first paragraph of the canon speaks of vicariates and prefectures apostolic, not of dioceses. The second paragraph of the canon begins with references to councils in a rather analogous sense.[33] But then the canon specifically mentions provincial councils and states that there is no determined time for their celebration. Hence, an ecclesiastical province is apparently supposed here.[34]

It seems, however, that the norm of canon 304, § 2, can be considered applicable also to mission places where metropolitans do not exist. Winslow [35] describes quasi-provincial councils, consisting of groups of vicariates and prefectures apostolic, which were celebrated in China. Vermeersch-Creusen [36] also admit the possibility of such

[29] Wernz-Vidal, *loc. cit.*: "Ubi in regione nulla est provincia ecclesiastica erecta evidenter nec Concilium plenarium aut regionale nec Concilium provinciale haberi potest."

[30] *Enchiridion Iuris Canonici* (2. ed., Pécs: Ex Typographia "Haladas R. T.," 1931), p. 229, note 12.

[31] *Inst.*, I, 437.

[32] *Ius de Personis*, p. 299.

[33] Canon 304, § 2: Pariter quae de Conciliis plenariis et provincialibus can. 281-291 praescribuntur, *applicari debent, congrua congruis referendo* . . . in regionibus . . . (Italics are the writer's.)

[34] Vermeersch-Creusen, *Epitome*, I, 326.

[35] *Vicars and Prefects Apostolic*, The Catholic University of America Canon Law Studies, n. 24 (Washington, D. C.: The Catholic University of America, 1924), p. 50. Cf. *infra*, p. 92, note 12.

[36] *Epitome*, I, 327.

councils (which they term regional), which however they consider to be lacking in jurisdiction, apart from the previous permission of the Holy See for their celebration. This is substantially the explanation of Chelodi,[37] who stated that a mandate from the Holy See is required.

Toso [38] makes a distinction which is worthy of note, namely, that if the entire province to which a vicariate or prefecture apostolic belongs is subject to the Sacred Congregation for the Propagation of the Faith, there is no fixed time for the celebration of councils; but, if the province to which the vicariate or prefecture belongs is subject to the Sacred Consistorial Congregation, then the provisions of canon 283 concerning the regular celebration of provincial councils are to be observed.

It appears, then, that canon 304, § 2, both regulates the celebration of councils by metropolitans and also makes provision for an institution similar to councils in regions subject to the Sacred Congregation for the Propagation of the Faith. Metropolitans who are subject to this Congregation cannot convoke provincial councils without the permission of the Congregation, and there is no fixed time for the convocation. Canon 304, § 2, should be regarded as stating an exception to canon 283.

1. Is There a Contrary Custom?

It is only with the consent of the competent ecclesiastical superior that customary usage obtains the force of an ecclesiastical law.[39] However, it is not required that the legislator express his consent in words or in writing. If a usage of sufficiently long standing is a public matter so that he can readily know about it, it suffices that he give his consent tacitly through not opposing the formative usage by means of some public act whenever he was able to do so.[40] By a single act, however, the legislator can manifest his contrary will, and so interrupt the otherwise prescriptive force inherent in long

[37] *Ius de Personis,* p. 299.
[38] *Commentaria Minora,* III, 125, 126.
[39] Canon 25.
[40] Michiels, *Normae Generales,* II, 31; Coronata, *Inst.,* I, 40.

continued usage as a potential agency for supplanting extant law. He may oppose an existing usage by publicly denouncing it, by bringing the law's violators to trial or punishment, or by reprobating future usages and practices that run counter to some determined law.[41]

The turbulent political conditions and other factors which conspired against the regular celebration of provincial councils in the post-Tridentine era have been outlined in a previous chapter.[42] That the Popes always favored the celebration of councils is clear; [43] but whether they gave tacit consent to the complete non-observance of the law in many regions is another question.[44] Pre-Code authors generally admitted some mitigation of the law, so far as the prescribed triennial celebration was concerned.[45] But that the obligation of celebrating councils had lapsed by way of complete abrogation was not generally maintained. It was held that the complete foregoing of the celebration of councils did stand as a legitimate custom, but existed rather as a corruption of the law [46] or as the result of political circumstances which prevented the observance of the law according to the will of the legislator.[47]

However, the question regarding the existence of a contrary custom has been settled effectively by the Code,[48] since the establishment of a new law is one way of revoking a contrary custom.[49] A new law with entirely new terms is in force.

[41] Michiels, *ibid.*, p. 39; cf. canon 27, § 1.

[42] Cf. *supra*, Chapter II, Article 2.

[43] Cf. *supra*, pp. 27, 28, notes 33 and 36.

[44] Smith (*Elements of Ecclesiastical Law* [3 vols., Vol. I, 7. ed., completely revised according to the decrees of the Third Plenary Council of Baltimore, New York, 1887], I, 35) stated that very few councils were held throughout three centuries, and the Holy See seemed to have given tacit consent to this.

[45] Craisson, *Manuale Juris Canonici* (4 vols., 6. ed., Pictavii, 1880), I, 47; Santi-Leitner, *Praelectiones Juris Canonici* (5 vols. in 3, 4. ed., Ratisbonae, 1903-1905), I, n. 153.

[46] Santi-Leitner, *loc. cit.* Cf. Benedictus XIV, *De Syn.*, Lib. I, cap. 6, n. 5.

[47] Bouix, *De Concilio Provinciali*, pp. 38-53.

[48] Cf. canon 283, which requires provincial councils to be held every twenty years, in contrast to the Tridentine law calling for a triennial celebration; Wernz-Vidal, II, p. 679, note 39.

[49] Michiels, *Normae Generales*, II, 39; cf. canon 5.

Even if it were granted that before the advent of the present Code the legislator had given his tacit consent to the complete cessation of the celebration of provincial councils, only the pre-Code existence of an immemorial or centenary custom could be urged against the present law of the Code, and then only on the condition that this contrary custom could not be prudently removed after the enactment of the Code.[50] If, therefore, in any given province a provincial council had been celebrated even but once within the century before the promulgation of the present Code, there would be no juridical basis for the plea that in such a province an established contrary custom could do away with the need of conforming to the law as now enacted in the Code.

Obviously, a custom contrary to canon 283 has not been established since the time of the Code, for that fact would involve two conditions beyond present realization:

(1) A contrary usage of forty continuous and uninterrupted years calculated from a date no earlier than May 19, 1938.[51] Canon 283 requires that a council be celebrated in each ecclesiastical province at least once within a period of twenty years. The Code therefore enacted the obligation of celebrating the requisite provincial councils at least once between May 19, 1918 and May 19, 1938. Hence only from the latter (or some subsequent) date could it be said that the law of canon 283 had been first violated or that a usage contrary to canon 283 had been initiated.

(2) The consent of the Holy Father.[52] The supreme legislator's legal consent, as contained in canon 27, would indeed suffice for the

[50] Cf. canon 5. Cf. Vermeersch-Creusen, *Epitome*, I, 72.

[51] Canon 27 states that a contrary usage cannot supplant an ecclesiastical law unless that usage be reasonable in character and have at the same time, as a potential agency with legally prescriptive force, run a course of forty continuous and uninterrupted years. Cf. Woywod, *A Practical Commentary on the Code of Canon Law* (2 vols., New York: Wagner, Vol. I, 6. printing, 1941; Vol. II, 5. ed. revised, 1939), I, 16.

[52] Canon 25: Consuetudo in Ecclesia vim legis a consensu competentis Superioris ecclesiastici unice obtinet.

furnishing of juridical efficacy to a usage contrary to the common law, but this legal consent is accorded only then when the conditions of canon 27 are completely satisfied.[53]

2. Do Episcopal Conferences Supply for Councils?

The conferences of the bishops of each province every five years are prescribed in canon 292. Herein the Code has introduced a new law, which supplements the requirement for celebrating councils and compensates for the longer interval between provincial councils.[54] But an episcopal conference is only a consultative meeting. It lacks collective jurisdiction and so cannot enact laws for the province.[55]

The mutual counsel which these conferences involve is of assistance in the meeting and expediting of common administrative difficulties and local problems, provides cooperation among the bishops, and favors and prepares the way for the subsequent provincial councils.[56] But the resolutions formulated in these gatherings take effect only in so far as they are personally adopted and promulgated by the individual bishops in their own dioceses.

Thus episcopal conferences may be said to prepare the way for the uniform government of the province, but they alone cannot accomplish this, since they lack the jurisdiction which belongs to provincial councils.

[53] Cf. Guilfoyle, *Custom,* The Catholic University of America Canon Law Studies, n. 105 (Washington, D. C.: The Catholic University of America, 1937), p. 83; Vermeersch-Creusen, *Epitome,* I, 130. If the legislator by even a single public act manifests his will against an existing usage he thereby interrupts the otherwise prescriptive force inherent in such usage as a potential agency for supplanting extant law. Cf. *supra,* pp. 81, 82.

[54] Wernz-Vidal, II, p. 679, note 39.

[55] Chelodi, *Ius de Personis,* p. 387; Oesterle, *Praelectiones Iuris Canonici,* I, 157. The Code contains two exceptions: canons 1507, § 1, and 1909, § 1, authorize episcopal confertnces, in lieu of a provincial council, to regulate the payment of fees and offerings as called for in the province.

[56] Cf. canon 292, §§ 1, 3. Cf. also Ferreres, *Institutiones Canonicae* (2 vols., 2. ed. correctior et tutior, Barcinone, 1920), I, n. 599.

B. *Saltem*

The Code determines the minimum requirement relative to the frequency with which provincial councils are to be held. May a metropolitan convoke councils oftener than once every twenty years? The present law, as also the Tridentine law,[57] was enacted, not to impede a more frequent celebration of councils, but to prevent all undue postponement in this important matter. The word *"saltem"* in the texts of both the present and the former law indicates this clearly, as does the whole background of the present legislation.[58]

Evidently, however, the right of the metropolitan to convoke councils must be placed within prescribed limits, since otherwise the rights of the suffragan bishops, who are obliged by the convocation, could be subject to infringement. The conclusion is clear: the celebration of councils oftener than once in twenty years depends upon the consent of a majority of those who have a decisive vote at the council. This conclusion is rendered firm by canon 288, which provides that even the protracting of a council which is in session requires the consent of the Fathers of the council.[59]

Article 3. Selection of the Place for the Council

Can 284. Metropolita, eoque legitime impedito vel sede archiepiscopali vacante, Suffraganeus antiquior promotione ad ecclesiam suffraganeam:

1°. Locum ad celebrandum Concilium intra provinciae territorium, auditis omnibus qui assistere debent cum suffragio deliberativo, eligit; cessantibus tamen iustis impedimentis, metropolitana ecclesia ne negligatur . . .

[57] Cf. Sebastianelli, *Praelectiones Juris Canonici* (3 vols., Vol. I, *De Personis*, 2. ed. emendata et aucta, Romae, 1905), I, 157.

[58] Cf. *supra*, pp. 3-9, 23, 24.

[59] Cf. Blat, *Commentarium*, II, 254. Under the Tridentine law, councils were required at least once in each period of three years. To convoke provincial councils more frequently than this required the consent of the suffragan bishops. Cf. Petra, *Commentaria*, I, p. 276, n. 12.

The exact time for the celebration of the council is left undetermined in the law, and so rests with the judgment of the metropolitan. Similarly, the choice of the place for the celebration of the council ultimately rests with the metropolitan, but in this case there are definite prescriptions of law which must be observed. Those who have a right to a deliberative vote at the council also have a right to be heard before the metropolitan makes his decision concerning the place for the council's celebration. This is the import of the phrase, "*auditis omnibus qui assistere debent cum suffragio deliberativo.*"[60]

But what if the metropolitan should violate that right and proceed to convoke a council without consulting his brother prelates? When the law states that by words such as "*audito Capitulo*" a superior needs the counsel of certain persons in order to act, it suffices for validity that the superior receive the counsel of these persons.[61] This prescript of canon 105, 1°, according to the more common teaching of canonists,[62] expresses a condition for validity. According to the forceful arguments of Ojetti,[63] validity is the point at issue, for otherwise the words "*indigere consilio*" and "*ad valide agendum*" would appear to be superfluous. Especially the latter phrase, "in order to act validly," seems to establish a condition for validity, namely, the required counsel. However, since the contrary opinion finds support among some outstanding canonists[64] who assert that

[60] Canon 284, 1°.

[61] Canon 105: Cum ius statuit Superiorem ad agendum *indigere* [italics by the writer] consilio aliquarum personarum:

1° . . . si consilium tantum [exigatur], per verba, ex. gr.: *de consilio consultorum, vel audito Capitudo, parocho*, etc., satis est ad *valide* [italics by the writer] agendum ut Superior illas personas audiat . . .

[62] Cf. Coronata, *Inst.*, I, p. 172, note 8; Ojetti, *Commentarium in Codicem Iuris Canonici* (4 vols. in 3, Romae: Apud Aedes Universitatis Gregorianae, 1927-1931), II, 185-202; Chelodi, *Ius de Personis*, p. 180; Toso, *Commentaria Minora*, II, 54; Maroto, *Inst.*, I, 555; Beste, *Introductio in Codicem*, pp. 161, 162; Bastnagel, *The Appointment of Parochial Adjutants and Assistants*, The Catholic University of America Canon Law Studies, n. 58 (Washington, D. C.: The Catholic University of America, 1930), pp. 206-228.

[63] *Commentarium in Codicem Iuris Canonici*, II, 190-194.

[64] Cf. Vermeersch-Creusen, *Epitome*, I, 198-200; Wernz-Vidal, I, p. 42, note 25; Boudinhon, "Circa can. 105, n. 1, an nullus semper sit actus superioris non petito consilio"—*Jus Pontificum*, VIII (1928), 29-35; Creusen, "L'effet

what is sufficient for validity is not necessarily required for validity, it seems that until an authentic interpretation of canon 105, is given, a *dubium iuris* may be conceded to exist here.[65]

If, however, it should be established that canon 105, 1°, has invalidating force so far as the requirement of the seeking of counsel is concerned, would the failure of the metropolitan to obtain the opinion of his confrères invalidate his convocation of the council? It appears so to the writer within the limitations which follow, since the specification of the place is entirely necessary for the convention of the prelates.[66] An invalid convocation would not oblige the suffragans and other members to attend. However, the principles of convocation at elections, as set forth in canon 162, § 4, seem likewise to apply here. It appears that the actual presence of the prelates at the council, which would supply even for a failure to convoke them, would supply also for the failure to consult them concerning the place of the council, so far as the validity of the conciliar acts is concerned.

If it is necessary for the metropolitan to obtain the counsel of his confrères for the valid selection of the location for the holding of the provincial council, it touches also a point of validity that this counsel be obtained from the prelates, not only individually, or by letter, but in a meeting. This appears clearly from canon 105, 2°,[67]

juridique des consultations,"—*Nouvelle Revue Théologique* LV (1928), 100-116; Vromant, *De Bonis Ecclesiae Temporalibus* (2. ed., Louvain: Museum Lessianum, 1934), pp. 63-65; Claeys Boúúaert-Simenon, *Manuale Juris Canonici* (3 vols., Vol. I, 4. ed., Gandae et Leodii: Apud Seminarium, 1934), I, 153. Vermeersch-Creusen (*ibid.*, p. 199) mention, without indicating the sources, that Van Hove and Triebs (+ 1942) hold a similar liberal view. For a concise and masterly analysis of the arguments advanced by the proponents of the liberal doctrine, the reader is referred to Bastnagel (*The Appointment of Parochial Adjutants and Assistants*, pp. 206-228), who supports the contrary opinion.

[65] Beste, *ibid.*, p. 162.

[66] Cf. canons 162, § 1; 163. Cf. Coronata, *Inst.*, I, 251, 158.

[67] Canon 105, 2°: Si requiratur consensus vel consilium non unius tantum vel alterius personae, sed plurium simul, eae personae legitime convocentur, salvo praescripto can. 162, § 4, et mentem suam manifestent; Superior autem pro sua prudentia ac negotiorum gravitate potest eas adigere ad iusiurandum de secreto servando praestandum. The fact that canon 105, 2°, expresses a

which states that when several persons must be consulted, the consultation must follow the form of legitimate convocation and common deliberation. On this point there is little division among canonists, since they teach almost unanimously that common deliberation is required here for validity.[68]

Michiels [69] explains that the requirement for common deliberation as expressed in canon 105, 2°, extends not only to the case wherein the several persons to be consulted form a collegiate moral person, but also to that wherein they constitute merely a group or a *coetus*, such as the council of diocesan administration. This makes more understandable the application of this requirement in the present instance to the *coetus episcoporum*. Canon 105, 2°, states that the superior can bind the group to secrecy. This does not imply, as Michiels [70] well points out, that the members are bound to give their opinion by secret votes, since this is not stated in the law, and not infrequently would be opposed to useful discussion and to the free presenting of opinions.

With reference to the consultation of the Fathers concerning the place for the celebration of the council, the law offers two directions. First, the metropolitan church is to be preferred if it offers suitable accommodations and if its selection is not attended with serious inconveniences which would render another choice more reasonable.[71]

condition for validity seems clear from the phrase, "*salvo praescripto can.* 162, § 4." For it is precisely invalidity that is the concern of canon 162, § 4: Defectus convocationis non *obstat*, si praetermissi nihilominus interfuerint. (Emphasis added.)

[68] Cf. Chelodi, *loc. cit.;* Wernz-Vidal, II, 42, 43; Vermeersch-Creusen, *ibid.*, 200; Ojetti, *Commentarium in Codicem Iuris Canonici,* II, 182; Michiels (*De Personis,* pp. 428, 429), who states that common deliberation is necessary for validity, according to the more common and more probable opinion. The opposite opinion is held by Toso (*Commentaria Minora,* II, 54). Maroto (*Inst.,* I, p. 556, note 1) seemed inclined to admit exceptions from the requirement of common deliberation in view of a particular law or of an indult to the contrary.

[69] *De Personis,* p. 426.

[70] *De Personis,* pp. 429, 430.

[71] Canon 284, 1°; Fagnanus, Lib. V, tit. 1, cap. 25, n. 27. Cf. canon 357, § 2; Wernz-Vidal, II, 795.

Secondly, the place for the celebration of the council should be within the territory of the ecclesiastical province. This territory embraces the archdiocese and the dioceses of the suffragans, but does not extend to the territory of the exempt prelates who become affiliated with the metropolitan under the provisions of canon 285, since canon 285 does not imply a territorial annexation of their jurisdictions to the province.[72]

In selecting the place for the holding of the council the metropolitan should show deference for the opinion of the Fathers, and especially so if it be unanimous, but he remains free, according to his own prudent judgment, to decide the matter independently of their manifested proposal.[73] Fagnanus [74] advises that in making his choice the metropolitan should show consideration for the distances to be traveled by his confrères, and accordingly should not select a place too remote.

[72] Cf. canons 272 and 215, § 1.

[73] Cf. canon 105, 1°. Cf. also Toso, *Commentaria Minora*, III, 106.

[74] *Commentaria in Quinque Decretalium Libros*, Lib. V, tit. 1, cap. 25, n. 26.

CHAPTER VI

CELEBRATION OF THE PROVINCIAL COUNCIL

Article 1. Members Having a Deliberative Vote

A. Deliberative Vote Granted by Law

Of the prelates who enjoy a decisive vote at provincial councils, some occupy a territory which is included within the geographical confines of a province erected by the Holy See. Other prelates, as described in canon 285, although they reside outside the province, become affiliated with it by electing the metropolitan as their own, with the approval of the Holy See. Procurators are invested with the right of taking a decisive vote only if they are at the same time coadjutor or auxiliary bishops to the ordinary whom they represent at the council.

1. Local Ordinaries

As exercising territorial jurisdiction, provincial councils are comprised of local ordinaries [1] who have ordinary powers of jurisdiction in the territory which is subject to the conciliar decrees. The vicars general of these ordinaries are not included here, since a vicar general is merely an *alter ego,* is or is not appointed in a territory, according to varying circumstances, at the discretion of the prelate,[2] and exer-

[1] Local ordinaries are prelates who exercise ordinary jurisdiction (as contrasted with delegated jurisdiction—cf. canon 197, § 1) over a territory in both the internal and the external forum. Primarily and directly their jurisdiction extends over a territory; only secondarily does it relate to the persons residing in the territory. Local ordinaries are thus distinguished from religious ordinaries, whose jurisdiction directly apples to persons, and not primarily to a place. Cf. Wernz-Vidal, II, 427.

[2] Canon 366, § 1, indicates that a diocese ordinarily should have at least one vicar general. Cf. canons 294, § 1, and 323, § 3, concerning the appointment of a vicar general in other territories. Cf. Wernz-Vidal, II, 690, 691.

cises his jurisdictional powers with dependence upon the will of his proper ordinary.[3]

Thus the law does not grant vicars general or other persons concomitant and equal rights with their bishops in deciding provincial matters, especially since the rights not merely of one but of all of the prelates are involved in the determining of provincial decrees. These mutual rights of the prelates are protected by the law which imposes upon the metropolitan the obligation of calling all the members to the council.[4] The territories which will be ruled by the council's decrees are protected by the law which imposes upon the prelates the obligation to participate in the fashioning of the decrees.[5]

a. Residing Within the Province

Canon 286, § 1. Praeter Episcopos, Abbates vel Praelatos *nullius* et Archiepiscopos de quibus in can. 285, ad Concilium provinciale vocandi sunt et convenire debent cum voto deliberativo Suffraganei omnes aliique de quibus in can. 282, § 1.

Canon 282, § 1. Concilio plenario assistere debent cum suffragio deliberativo, praeter Legatum Apostolicum, Metropolitae, Episcopi residentiales, qui, sui loco, mittere possunt Coadiutorem vel Auxiliarem, Apostolici dioecesium Administratores, Abbates vel Praelati *nullius*, Vicarii Apostolici, Praefecti Apostolici, Vicarii Capitulares.

The jurisdiction of local ordinaries arises along with their taking canonical possession of their office. The usual manner prescribed for taking possession of office consists in the presentation of the apostolic letters of appointment, either by the person appointed or

[3] Cf. canon 369, § 2. If the vicar general should receive full powers of administration over a diocese according to the norms of canons 429 or 432, he would then possess (as will be shown) a deliberative vote at the provincial council.

[4] Canon 286, § 1: . . . vocandi sunt . . .

[5] Canon 286, § 1: . . . convenire debent . . .

by his duly determined proxy,[6] to the competent authority of the territory, as specified in law.[7] Special provisions of law govern the establishment of succession to local jurisdiction, *sede impedita*[8] or *sede vacante.*[9] It is the possession of local jurisdiction, and not the previous reception of episcopal consecration, that determines the right of local ordinaries to be members of the council.[10] Consequently, suffragan bishops who have not yet been consecrated but who have taken the canonical possession of their office must be invited as full members of the conciliar assembly. Obviously, the same principle holds true for the other local ordinaries under consideration, since often they are not bishops at all.

The enumeration of the local ordinaries includes the metropolitan and suffragan bishops, apostolic administrators of dioceses,[11] vicars and prefects apostolic,[12] and vicars capitular[13]—all of whom rule a diocese or a vicariate or prefecture apostolic within the province.[14]

Canon 282, § 1, as applied to provincial councils, does not include the apostolic legate, since in that exclusive status he is not consti-

[6] Canon 1445: Possessio beneficii etiam per procuratorem, speciale mandatum habentem, capi potest.

[7] Cf. canons 334, § 3; 353; 293, § 1; 322, § 1; 313.

[8] Cf. canons 429; 327, § 2; 309, § 2.

[9] Cf. canons 432; 355; 327, § 1; 317.

[10] Cf. Wernz-Vidal (II, 677), who stated this principle concerning suffragan bishops.

[11] Canon 312: Dioecesis canonice erectae regimen, sive plena, sive vacante sede, aliquando Summus Pontifex ob graves et speciales causas Administratori Apostolico vel in perpetuum vel ad tempus committit.

[12] De Meester (II, 120) defined vicars and prefects apostolic as follows: "Vicarii et Praefecti Apostolici sunt Praelati ecclesiastici a Sede Apostolica nominati, qui in regione ubi hierarchia nunquam exstitit, vel nondum restituta est, vel inchoatum aliquid adhuc secumfert, ad munia apostolica sub auctoritate S. C. de Prop. Fide exercenda, vices S. Pontificis agant." De Meester, *ibid.*, note 2: "Nominantur a S. C. Consist., si erectio novae Praefecturae Apostolicae aut novi Vicariatus apostolici fit per dismembrationem dioecesis iam existentis; omnes alii nominantur per S. C. de Prop. Fide."

[13] A vicar capitular is the local ordinary of a territory, *sede vel abbatia vel praelatura vacante.* He is elected as the vicar of the *capitulum.* Cf. canon 432, §§ 1, 3. Cf. also Wernz-Vidal, II, 899, 900.

[14] Cf. Wernz-Vidal, II, 678.

tuted a local ordinary.[15] The context of canon 282, § 1, compared with that of canon 281, leaves no room for doubt that the phrase "*praeter Legatum Apostolicum*" applies only to plenary and not to provincial councils.[16]

Canon 282, § 1, does not apparently intend to exclude (with the exception of vicars general) any local ordinaries who exercise full jurisdiction over a territory which is subject to the conciliar decrees, but who are called by a name other than one of those enumerated in the canon under consideration. Coadjutor bishops who rule a diocese with full jurisdiction are not specifically mentioned in the canon, but authors [17] include them among the members who hold the right of a deliberative vote. It does not appear that exception can be taken to this view, since such coadjutor bishops seem to be at least not inferior in office to apostolic administrators, of whom specific mention is made in canon 282, § 1.[18]

Vermeersch-Creusen teach that the listing in canon 282, § 1, extends to all local ordinaries, except vicars general.[19] The conclusion would follow that, when the jurisdiction of the vicar or prefect apostolic has ceased or is impeded, pro-vicars and pro-prefects apostolic, for instance, would have the right to be invited with the possession of a decisive vote, since they are constituted local ordinaries by the law.[20] The view of Vermeersch-Creusen, although not ex-

[15] Cf. canons 269, § 1, and 198.

[16] This is also clear from the constant practice of provincial councils; cf. *supra*, pp. 18, 19. Moreover, it is not the apostolic legate but the metropolitan who convokes and presides at provincial councils. Cf. canons 284, § 2; 281.

[17] Wernz-Vidal, II, 678; Vermeersch-Creusen, *Epitome*, I, 313.

[18] Coadjutor bishops who possess full powers of diocesan administration are in the present work regarded as local ordinaries. Cf. Lynch, *Coadjutors and Auxiliaries of Bishops*, pp. 75, 76.

[19] *Epitome, loc. cit.*

[20] Canon 309, § 2. Pro-vicars and pro-prefects apostolic have *sede vacante* or *sede impedita* the right to administer the Sacrament of Confirmation and they enjoy also all other rights which in the law are accorded to vicars and prefects apostolic. Cf. Winslow, *Vicars and Prefects Apostolic*, p. 65; Coleman, *The Minister of Confirmation*, The Catholic University of America Canon Law Studies, n. 125 (Washington, D. C.: The Catholic University of America Press, 1941), pp. 121, 122.

pressed by other authors, appears to be tenable. For the force of the law on conciliar membership seems to mean that each territory which is recognized by the Holy See as a constituent subject of a particular province's laws should have its ordinary as a personal representative, a voting member at the council.[21]

The question may be raised, however, whether it is not an extension of the law to understand as equivalent to *"Vicarii Capitulares,"* who are constituted in office only *sede vacante,* those who succeed in the government *sede impedita tantum.* For in the case of vicars capitular, the original prelate's jurisdiction has been terminated by the vacancy of the see,[22] while in that of the priest who is constituted an ordinary when the see or the equivalent territorial jurisdiction is merely impeded the original prelate's jurisdiction has not been terminated, but has simply been rendered incapable of being exercised.[23]

The distinction of *sede impedita* and *sede vacante* appears to exist in the law rather to restrict the assumption of the government of the see by the cathedral chapter, than to constitute the successor to the government *sede impedita* as inferior in rights or jurisdiction to the vicar capitular. For the law of the Code gives the same jurisdiction to the one as to the other,[24] and should the administrator *sede impedita* be himself impeded, then the cathedral chapter must elect a vicar, who rules the diocese with the power of a vicar capitular.[25]

Moreover, the context of canon 282, § 1, which grants a deliberative vote to a coadjutor or auxiliary bishop who acts as a proxy for his bishop, seems to express the principle that each territory subject to the provincial council should be represented at the council. But *sede impedita* such representation at the provincial council can be exercised only through the administrator who is constituted a local

[21] Toso (*Commentaria Minora,* III, 105) reasons in a similar fashion concerning the deliberative vote which is accorded to apostolic administrators. Cf. decree 60, note 6, of the II Plenary Council of Baltimore (1866)—*Coll. Lac.,* III, 417, d.

[22] Cf. canon 432, § 1.

[23] Cf. canons 429, § 1; 327, § 2; 317; 309, §§ 2, 4.

[24] Cf. canons 429, § 1, and 432, § 1. Cf. Wernz-Vidal, II, 896.

[25] Cf. canon 429, § 3.

ordinary by the law.[26] That the law does not intend to exclude such local ordinaries is also supported by the fact of the express mention of *locorum Ordinarii* in canon 292, § 1, which is explained as a parallel canon to canon 282, § 1.[27]

It may be stated, therefore, that all local ordinaries, except vicars general, appear to have a deliberative vote at provincial councils.

b. Residing Outside the Province

Bishops who are exempt from any dependence upon a metropolitan and are immediately subject to the Holy See are called "exempt bishops."[28] The Council of Trent provided that such bishops, while retaining their privileges and exemptions, should select a neighboring metropolitan, and then have the obligation of participating in his provincial councils and of effecting in their own diocese the observance of the conciliar decrees. The Tridentine decree read as follows:

> *Itidem episcopi, qui nulli archiepiscopo subiiciuntur, aliquem vicinum metropolitanum semel eligant, in cuius Synodo provinciali cum aliis interesse debeant; et quae ibi ordinata fuerint, observent, ac observari faciant. In reliquis omnibus eorum exemptio et privilegia salva atque integra maneant.*[29]

Canon 285 of the present Code, while retaining substantially the Tridentine legislation, has made certain changes. Canon 285 reads as follows:

> *Episcopi qui nulli Metropolitae subiiciuntur, Abbates vel Praelati* NULLIUS, *et Archiepiscopi Suffraganeis carentes, ali-*

[26] Canon 198, § 1: In iure nomine *Ordinarii* intelliguntur . . . itemque ii qui praedictis deficientibus interim ex iuris praescripto . . . succedunt in regimine . . .

2. Nomine autem *Ordinarii loci* seu *locorum* veniunt omnes recensiti, exceptis Superioribus religiosis.

[27] Cf. Vermeersch-Creusen, *Epitome*, I, 315. Canons 292, § 2, and 285 are expressly stated as being connected; canons 292, § 1, and 282, § 1, complete the parallel. Cf. also canon 281.

[28] Vermeersch-Creusen, *Epitome*, I, 338.

[29] Sess. XXIV, *de ref.*, c. 2.

quem viciniorem Metropolitam, nisi forte iam elegerint, semel pro semper, praevia Sedis Apostolicae approbatione, eligant, cuius Concilio provinciali cum aliis intersint, et quae ibi ordinata fuerint, observent et observanda curent.

The mention of abbots and prelates *nullius* [30] and of archbishops who lack suffragans is a new feature. Once an exempt prelate has made the choice of a metropolitan, with the Holy See's approval, it is to be considered final and irrevocable by any succeeding prelate. This is indicated by the emphasis of the phrase *semel pro semper* as contrasted with the single word *semel* of the former legislation. Moreover, the previous approbation of the Holy See is now a *conditio sine qua non* for the validity of the choice.

The decisive vote which belongs to the exempt prelates, their essential right of becoming invited, and their strict obligation of attending the provincial council, are clearly stated in canon 286, § 1.[31] Toso [32] observes that especially in Italy are to be found large numbers of exempt prelates as archbishops *honoris causa* and as bishops who are immediately subject to the Holy See.[33]

Apostolic administrators of dioceses, vicars apostolic, and even (although rarely) prefects apostolic are sometimes bishops who are immediately subject to the Holy See, and thus are without dependence on any metropolitan.[34] Could any of these ordinaries be classified as among the exempt bishops mentioned in canon 285? Authors do not expressly consider this question. However, in the case of apostolic administrators it is to be remembered that they have the

[30] Canon 319, § 1: Praelati qui praesunt territorio proprio, separato ab omni dioecesi, cum clero et populo, dicuntur Abbates vel Praelati *nullius,* nempe dioecesis, prout eorum ecclesia dignitate abbatiali vel simpliciter praelatitia gaudet. (The laws of the Code refer solely to abbacies or prelacies *nullius* which consist of at least three parishes. Cf. canon 319, § 2.)

[31] Canon 286, § 1: Praeter Episcopos, Abbates vel Praelatos *nullius* et Archiepiscopos de quibus in can. 285, ad Concilium provinciale vocandi sunt et convenire debent cum voto deliberativo Suffraganei omnes aliique de quibus in can. 282, § 1.

[32] *Commentaria Minora,* III, 107.

[33] Cf. Gams, *Series Episcoporum,* I, 659, and I, 257, for enumerations of exempt sees.

[34] Wernz-Vidal, II, 701, 696.

administration of a canonically erected diocese, which has already been established in a given province.[35] Hence the apostolic administrator governs a see which belongs to a definite province, and thus canon 285 remains without application in the case.[36]

With vicars and prefects apostolic the case is not so clear. Toso [37] seems to imply that they may at times come under the provisions of canon 285, for he refers canons 282, § 1, 285, and 286, § 1, to vicars and prefects apostolic. The contrary inference seems to have been made by Wernz-Vidal, for they considered vicars and prefects apostolic as residing within the ecclesiastical province.[38] When vicars apostolic are bishops, they are only titular bishops, and hence do not govern an exempt see. For that reason, and since they are under the specific instructions of the Sacred Congregation for the Propagation of the Faith, it does not appear that vicars or prefects apostolic are included under the provisions of canon 285.

The metropolitan to be elected by the exempt prelate is now designated as *viciniorem* rather than (as in the former law) *vicinum*. Blat [39] declares that the greater proximity is the norm of the choice. However, the meaning of the phrase does not appear to be the "nearest metropolitan," for *vicinissimum* is not used. Nor does the expression mean the "nearer metropolitan," for the indefinite pronominal adjective *aliquem* is connected with it. Moreover, there is question of a choice to be made. The canon does not rigidly determine who the neighboring metropolitan is, nor is it the policy of the Holy See to exact the requirement that the selective option warranted in canon 285 be resolved into a mere computation of comparative distances.[40]

[35] Canon 312.

[36] Only the Holy See can change a territory in its pertinence from one province to another. Cf. canon 215.

[37] *Commentaria Minora*, III, 126.

[38] *Ius Canonicum*, II, 678: ". . . Vicarii et Praefecti Apostolici, qui Vicariatum aut Praefecturam Apostolicam intra provinciam regunt."

[39] *Commentarium*, II, 255.

[40] Cf. Augustine (*Commentary*, II, 301), who mentioned the increasingly liberal practice of the Holy See in this matter.

In the opinion of the writer, the expression, "one of the neighboring metropolitans," is a fair translation of the text.[41] Benko[42] points out that traveling facilities as well as distances must be considered. The essential and canonical aspect of this choice is the Holy See's ultimate approval of it. Once the choice has been canonically made and approved it is not subject to change, so that any future questions concerning the application of canon 285 are removed.[43]

2. Procurators, if Coadjutor or Auxiliary Bishops

Canon 282, § 1, makes a special concession in favor of bishops who have a coadjutor or auxiliary and are personally impeded from attending the council. It is stated that they can send their coadjutor or auxiliary bishop in their own place and with the privilege of a deliberative vote.[44]

Under the present law these are the only procurators who have a decisive vote at provincial councils. The reason for this concession may be founded in the fact that a bishop's need of a coadjutor or auxiliary bishop is often connected with the burden of ill health or of advancing years, so that there is a greater likelihood in his case that he may be justly impeded from participating in the council

[41] Cf. Woywod, *A Practical Commentary on the Code of Canon Law*, I, 107. The Latin comparative often has the force of moderating rather than strengthening the positive form of the adjective, so that the phrase *aliquem viciniorem Metropolitam* could mean "some metropolitan rather near." Cf. Bennett, *New Latin Grammar* (Boston, New York, Chicago, 1918), n. 240.

[42] *The Abbot* NULLIUS, The Catholic University of America Canon Law Studies, n. 173 (Washington, D. C.: The Catholic University of America Press, 1943), p. 95.

[43] Blat, *Commentarium,* II, 255. The electing of the metropolitan, in accordance with canon 285, has other juridical effects, as delineated in canons 429, § 5; 432, § 3; 1594, § 3. Cf. Coronata, *Inst.*, I, 426.

[44] Canon 282, § 1, indicates that all persons enumerated have a decisive vote. Before the Code, it was only with the consent of the council that a procurator could exercise a deliberative vote. Cf. *supra,* p. 27, note 30; Petra, *Commentaria,* I, p. 279, n. 39.

personally. The bishop should give his procurator a special written mandate to act in his stead,[45] and should address to the Fathers of the council a letter certifying the legitimate reasons for his absence.[46]

B. Deliberative Vote Accorded by Authority

Canon 286, § 2. Episcopi titulares qui in provincia degunt, possunt a praeside, cum consensu maioris partis illorum qui voto deliberativo intersunt, convocari, et si convocentur, votum habent deliberativum, nisi aliud in convocatione caveatur.

Titular bishops who reside in the province by reason of having within the province a domicile or a quasi-domicile[47] can be invited to the council with the effect of enjoying the right of deliberative vote, but for their invitation the consent of the majority of the council must first be obtained.[48] The final clause of canon 286, § 2, indicates that the Fathers may decide to invite a titular bishop without granting him a deliberative vote. But this restriction must be explicitly manifested in the letter of convocation, since otherwise the invitation implies that the titular bishop has a decisive vote Coronata teaches that a titular bishop has not the right to send a procurator.[49]

[45] Cf. canon 1659, § 1; Petra, *loc. cit.*

[46] Cf. canon 287, § 1; Blat, *Commentarium,* II, 257; S. C. C. *Tarraconen.,* 4 dec. 1638—*Fontes,* n. 2596; cf. *infra,* pp. 106, 107. For further details concerning procurators, cf. *infra,* pp. 100-105.

[47] Vermeersch-Creusen (*Epitome,* II, 313) explain that the term *degunt* embodies the requirement of having at least a quasi-domicile in the province. It is to be noted that a domicile or a quasi-domicile can be acquired, not in a province as such, but only in reference to a diocese, vicariate, prefecture, parish or quasi-parish. Cf. canon 92, § 1.

[48] The former law required the unanimous consent of the council. Cf. S. C. C., *Aquen.,* 24 aug. 1850, ad I—*Fontes,* n. 4112.

[49] *Inst.,* I, 426, note 6.

Article 2. Persons Having a Consultative Vote

A. Procurators

Canon 287, § 1. Qui Concilio provinciali interesse debent cum voto deliberativo, si iusto impedimento detineantur, mittant procuratorem et impedimentum probent.

§ 2. Procurator, si fuerit unus ex Patribus quibus est votum deliberativum, duplici voto non gaudet; si non fuerit, habet votum dumtaxat consultivum.

Members to whom the right of a deliberative vote is granted by the law have the obligation of attending the provincial council.[50] But nowhere is the same obligation asserted for titular bishops, even when they are granted a decisive vote. Hence the obligation of sending a procurator does not apply to titular bishops. It applies only to the members who enjoy the right of a deliberative vote as granted by the law, for it is only upon them that the law imposes the obligation of personal attendance, conjoined with the alternative obligation of representation by proxy.[51] The principal must give his proxy a written mandate[52] and must address to the Fathers of the Council a letter establishing the existence of a just impediment, with reasons or documents that would persuade a prudent man.[53]

The person selected as proxy must be suited to the responsibility of giving advice before the conciliar body, and should be well informed on the state of the diocese. He should be commended by his prudence and should be a doctor of canon law or theology, or at

[50] Canon 286, § 1.

[51] Canon 287, § 1.

[52] Blat, *Commentarium*, II, 257.

[53] Canon 287, § 1; Blat, *loc. cit.* The judgment as to whether a legitimate impediment has been proved is committed to the Fathers of the council. Cf. S. C. C., *Tarraconen.*, 4 dec. 1638—*Fontes*, n. 2596.

least be well versed in those sciences.[54] One of the Fathers of the council may be chosen to act as a proxy for another members.[55]

The present law does not favor the practice of sending proxies. This is evidenced not only in the requirement set forth in the canon 287, § 1, that a just impediment must be proved, but also in the fact that procurators as such lack a vote, under the general comprehension of the law, unless the law specifically confers it upon them.[56] With the exception made in favor of bishops who send their own coadjutor or auxiliary as their proxy,[57] procurators are not given a deliberative vote.

If the procurator is one of the Fathers who has a deliberative vote, canon 287, § 2, states that he does not possess an additional vote as the representative of an absent bishop. McDonough [58] applies this canon to show that the temporary apostolic administrator of one diocese who is at the same time the residential bishop of another diocese has only a single vote at the council. Canon 287, § 2, provides, finally, that a procurator at provincial councils has a merely (*dumtaxat*) consultative vote, unless in his own right he enjoys a deliberative vote. The phrase, *votum duxtaxat consultivum,* and especially the restrictive word, *dumtaxat,* is of great importance, since it expresses a change from the former law, which permitted a deliberative vote to procurators of the absent Fathers, but only with

[54] S. C. C., *Tarraconen.*, 4 dec. 1638: ". . . Procuratores sint habiles, Doctores, et discreti."—*Fontes,* n. 2596. Cf. the qualifications required for the offices of the vicar general, the ruling official of the diocesan court, the promoter of justice, the defender of the bond, in canons 367, §§ 1, 2; 1573, § 4; 1589, § 1.

[55] Canon 287, § 2.

[56] Ferreres, *Institutiones Canonicae,* I, nn. 433, 594. Cf. canon 163: . . . convocatione legitime secuta, ius eligendi pertinet ad eos qui praesentes sunt die in convocatione statuto, exclusa facultate ferendi suffragia non solum per epistolam, sed etiam per procuratorem, nisi lege peculiari aliud caveatur.

[57] Canon 287, § 2.

[58] *Apostolic Administrators,* The Catholic University of America Canon Law Studies, n. 139 (Washington, D. C.: The Catholic University of America Press, 1941), pp. 132-134.

the consent of the Fathers of the council.[59] This change of legislation indicates, in the writer's opinion, an emphasis upon the obligation of attending the council personally. The far reaching consequences of councils postulate the need of the personal presence of the chief pastors of the flock.[60]

Could procurators be granted a deliberative vote on the grounds of an existing custom contrary to the Code? It is difficult for the writer to visualize circumstances in which canon 5 might be invoked in this case, for the reasons which follow. The issue is one in which the local ordinary, inferior to the Roman Pontiff, is not one of those persons who are enumerated in canon 198, since the matter involved is not diocesan but provincial in scope. Granted, however, that the provincial council corresponds to the *Ordinarii* mentioned in canon 5, two conditions would still be required:

(1) The council, by a majority vote, would be obliged to decide that the contrary custom of granting procurators a decisive vote could not be prudently removed in the light of the circumstances of places and persons. But the persons who are chiefly involved are local ordinaries (excluding vicars general), since they alone are entitled by law to vote and, in view of their personal obligation to support the law, there should be an additional presumption here in favor of the law over a contrary custom.

(2) It would be necessary for the custom to have been confirmed by the practice of at least two or three councils in the province (else it could scarcely be called a local custom) and, since the records of councils are not ordinarily lost to memory, it seems that only by a centenary custom could prescription occur in the present case.[61]

[59] Bouix, *De Concilio Provinciali,* p. 125. Decree 60 of the II Plenary Council of Baltimore (1866) provided that all procurators of absent Fathers were to be given a deliberative vote (cf. *Coll. Lac.*, III, 417, c), but this provision, as contrary to canon 287, § 2, is abrogated by the Code. Cf. canon 6, 2°.

[60] Procurators at ecumenical councils lack even a consultative vote (cf. canon 224, § 2). Blat (*Commentarium,* II, 257) asserts that one who has a deliberative vote does not acquire an additional consultative vote by acting as a proxy, since his counsel is expressed in his deliberative vote.

[61] Cf. canon 5. A custom may, however, remain immemorial in character, when it is so regarded by the community at large, even after a historical in-

B. Delegates of the Cathedral Chapter or of the Diocesan Consultors

Canon 286, § 3. Capitula cathedralia aut consultores dioecesani cuiusvis dioecesis cuius Ordinarius ad normam § 1 vocari debet, invitentur ad Concilium et invitati mittant duos ex capitularibus aut consultoribus collegialiter designatos, qui tamen obtinent votum tantum consultivum.

The cathedral chapter [62] or the body of diocesan consultors [63] command after the bishop the position of highest dignity in the diocese, since they are his senate and counsellors in the administration of the diocese and supply his place, *sede vacante*.[64] Because of their perpetual character as moral persons, they are the guardians and witnesses of the traditions of particular churches. And not infrequently provincial councils treat matters which are of concern to the cathedral chapter.

For these reasons, for every member of the council who has the right of a deliberative vote granted to him by law, the corresponding cathedral chapter or body of diocesan consultors must be invited by the metropolitan. The invitation is sent to them as a body, and they *collegialiter* appoint two deputies who represent them at the council with consultative votes.[65] Blat [66] offers the reminder that the chapters of the exempt prelates, described in canon 285, are also to be called to the council.

vestigation has brought to light the starting point of the custom. Cf. Vermeersch-Creusen, *Epitome*, I, 134.

The Fathers of the IV Provincial Council of Portland, Oregon (1932) recognized the existence of a custom contrary to the Code and granted a procurator a deliberative vote at the Council. Cf. *Acta et Decreta Concilii Provincialis Portlandensis in Oregon Quarti* (1932), p. 138, note.

[62] Cf. canon 391, § 1.

[63] Cf. canons 423, 427.

[64] Cf. canons 431, § 1; 432, § 1.

[65] Toso, *Commentaria Minora*, III, 108. Cf. canon 286, § 3.

[66] *Commentarium*, II, 256.

C. Major Superiors of Clerical Exempt Religious Communities and Superiors of Monastic Congregations

Canon 286, § 4. Maiores quoque religionum clericalium exemptarum ac Congregationum monasticarum Superiores, qui in provincia resideant, invitandi sunt, debentque invitati adesse aut impedimentum, quo detinentur, Concilio notum facere; sed his . . . votum est dumtaxat consultivum.

Among those to whom the law commands that an invitation be sent are religious ordinaries.[67] Religious clerical communities which enjoy the privilege of exemption are represented at provincial councils by their major superiors who reside in the province. Major superiors are enumerated in canon 488, 8°, which reads as follows:

> [*In canonibus qui sequuntur, veniunt nomine*] SUPERIORUM MAIORUM, *Abbas Primas, Abbas Superior Congregationis monasticae, Abbas monasterii sui iuris, licet ad monasticam Congregationem pertinentis, supremus religionis Moderator, Superior provincialis, eorundem vicarii aliique ad instar provincialium potestatem habentes.*

Each of these major superiors, if he belongs to a clerical exempt community, is also a religious ordinary, according to canon 198, § 1. Superiors of monastic congregations,[68] even if they are not abbots, as, for instance, conventual priors,[69] must be invited to provincial councils.[70]

[67] Cf. canons 286, § 4; 198, § 1; 488, 8°.

[68] Canon 488, 2°, defines a monastic congregation as the union of several monasteries *sui iuris* under the same superior. Cf. canons 501, § 3; 510; 516, § 1; 655, § 1; 1579, § 2; 1594, § 4. Cf. also Schaefer, *De Religiosis ad Normam Codicis Iuris Canonici* (3. ed. aucta et emendata, Romae: Typis Polyglottis Vaticanis, S. A. L. E. R., 1940), nn. 43 m; 51, § 7; 107, d; 145, a.

[69] Cf. Keene, *Religious Ordinaries and Canon* 198, The Catholic University of America Canon Law Studies, n. 135 (Washington, D. C.: The Catholic University of America Press, 1942), p. 2.

[70] Cf. canon 286, § 4. The opinion of Toso (*Commentaria Minora,* III, 108) that the abbot superior of a *single* monastery does not receive mention

Blat,[71] commenting upon the phrase *qui in provincia resideant,* remarks that by province is meant the ecclesiastical province over which the metropolitan presides,[72] and not the province of the religious with which the particular religious community is affiliated.[73] Hence only those major superiors who by reason of the office held by them reside in a religious house or monastery within the ecclesiastical province are to be called, so far as the obligation imposed by canon 286, § 4, is concerned.[74] It would be belaboring the obvious to explain that the obligatory presence of religious ordinaries at councils naturally follows from their knowledge of the rights and needs of their subjects and from their special qualifications, as leaders of the Church, to advise prudently and well.

D. Other Members of the Clergy

Of the persons thus far considered as attending provincial councils all are entitled by law to be invited except the titular bishops, whose invitation is at the option of the council. The Fathers of the council also have the full liberty to invite other members of the clergy who will possess a consultative vote.

From the ranks of both the religious and the diocesan clergy may be selected priests who will serve as theologians and canonists, or who will discharge the offices of the council, such as those of promoter, secretary, and notaries.[75] According to the usual practice, each prelate is accompanied by one or two theologians or canonists as his personal advisers.[76]

in canon 286, § 4, and hence lacks the right of a seat at the council, seems untenable, since he is in fact a major superior of a clerical exempt community. Cf. canon 488, 8°.

[71] *Commentarium,* II, 256.

[72] Cf. canon 272.

[73] Cf. canon 488, 6°.

[74] Blat, *loc. cit.*

[75] Bargilliat, *Praelectiones Juris Canonici* (28. ed. ab auctore recognita et recentioribus decretis accommodata, 2 vols., Parisiis, 1913), I, n. 680.

[76] Ojetti, *Synopsis Rerum Moralium et Iuris Pontificii* (2 vols. in 1, 2. ed., emendata et aucta, Prati, 1904-1905), "Concilium provinciale," p. 402. (Hereafter cited as *Synopsis.*)

ARTICLE 3. OBLIGATION OF ATTENDANCE

A. Obligation of Members Who Have a Deliberative Vote

Members who have a deliberative vote granted to them by the law are clearly bound to attend the council.[77] Not only must they present to the judgment of the council a just and reasonable excuse for their absence, but they have the further obligation of sending a procurator.[78]

The question may be raised whether the privilege accorded to residential bishops of sending their coadjutor or auxiliary as proxy exempts them from showing that a just impediment prevents their personal attendance at the council. Canon 287, § 1, states without exception the requirement that members who have the right of a deliberative vote granted to them by the law must prove the existence of a just impediment for their absence. Moreover, the denial of a deliberative vote to procurators indicates the legislator's will that the members should attend the council personally, when this is possible. The intent of the law is further manifested in the light of the pre-Code legislation which invoked specific penal sanctions in the event of an illegitimate absence.[79] Hence the phrase *mittere possunt* of canon 282, § 1, indicates a concession of law, not for sending a coadjutor when the bishop could attend the council in person, but for the granting of a deliberative vote to the coadjutor proxy when a just impediment is proved to exist in the principal.

Titular bishops, even when they are granted a deliberative vote, are not bound to attend the council, since this obligation is not stated in the law. Since their invitation is based, not on a legal right, but on a personal concession of the Fathers to them as indi-

[77] Cf. canon 282, § 1: . . . assistere debent . . .; canon 285: . . . cum aliis intersint . . .; canon 287, § 1: Qui Concilio plenario aut provinciali interesse debent cum voto deliberativo, si iusto impedimento detineantur, mittant procuratorem et impedimentum probent.

[78] Canon 287, § 2.

[79] Cf. *supra*, Chapter II, note 5.

viduals, titular bishops cannot extend their invitation to another person as their proxy.[80] It is only the members enjoying the right of a deliberative vote as granted to them by the law who have the right and obligation to be represented by a proxy.

B. Obligation of Persons Who Have a Consultative Vote

Major superiors of clerical exempt religious communities and superiors of monastic congregations clearly have the obligation of attending the council. Canon 286, § 4, states that they must be invited and must attend, or make known to the Fathers the reasonable excuse for their absence. Procurators are likewise bound to attend, since they take the place of members who have a deliberative vote granted to them by the law.

The law commands that the representatives of the cathedral chapter and of the diocesan consultors be invited to the council,[81] but according to the view of Vermeersch-Creusen they are not under the obligation of responding to the invitation.[82] This interpretation of canon 286, § 3, appeals to the fact that it is not positively stated that the chapters must come, or that they must manifest the just cause of their absence, whereas, by contrast, the very next paragraph of the canon imposes these explicit requirements upon the religious ordinaries. Vermeersch-Creusen understand the word *mittant* as indicating the way in which the cathedral chapters may respond to the invitation, namely, by sending two representatives, but not as imposing upon the chapters the obligation of thus sending them. These authors point to the former law under which cathedral chapters could not be compelled to come to the council,[83] and maintain that it has not been expressly changed by the Code.

[80] Cf. Coronata, *Inst.*, I, p. 426, note 6. Cf. Canons 223, § 2; 224, § 1; 359, § 1. Cf. also Vermeersch-Creusen, *Epitome*, I, 353; Wernz-Vidal, II, 792, 793.

[81] Canon 286, § 3: ". . . invitentur . . ."

[82] *Epitome*, I, 313, 314.

[83] C. 10, X, *de his quae fiunt a praelatis sine consensu capituli*, III, 10; Benedictus XIV, *De Syn.*, Lib. III, cap. 4, n. 1; Fagnanus, Lib. III, tit. 10, cap. 10, nn. 41, 42: Ojetti, *Synopsis*, "Concilium provinciale," p. 402.

Wernz-Vidal [84] Coronata [85] and Augustine [86] support the contrary opinion, namely, that the cathedral chapters and diocesan consultors have the obligation of sending two representatives to the council. This seems to the writer to be the only adequate explanation of the word *mittant*, which appears not to be equivalent to *mittere possunt*, but seems rather to express a command, "they shall send." Blat, referring to the major religious superiors who are necessarily to be invited, enunciates a principle which appears to be verified in regard to other persons who must be invited according to the law, namely, since they are necessarily to be called, so too they must correspond and attend.[87]

If this principle is applied to titular bishops [88] and to priests who have been freely invited,[89] it appears that, inasmuch as the law does not require that they be convoked, since there is no obligation to send them an invitation, they in turn remain free from the obligation of attending the council in the event that they are invited. Vermeersch-Creusen [90] teach that titular bishops are not under legal constraint to attend the council, and that thus there is no hardship imposed upon them should they have a domicile or a quasi-domicile in more than one province and receive invitations from more than one metropolitan. When the obligation of attending the council is

[84] *Ius Canonicum,* II, 678.

[85] *Inst.,* I, 426.

[86] *Commentary,* II, 302.

[87] *Commentarium,* II, 256: ". . . *invitandi sunt,* quod dicitur praescriptive, ipsi pariter (b) *debentque invitati adesse,* sed ratione impedimenti forsan existentis additur: (c) *aut impedimentum, quo detinentur, Concilio notum facere,* atque hoc iussum est, nec sine causa, eo quod obligatorie vocantur ac de spretu possent conqueri, sic Concilium videat num e contra spretus ab eis vel parvipensio fiat . . ."

[88] Cf. canon 286, § 2: Episcopi titulares qui in provincia degunt *possunt* . . . convocari . . . (Italics are the writer's.)

[89] Cf. canon 286, § 4: . . . aliis ex utroque clero viris ad Concilium *forte* vocatis. (Italics are the writer's.)

[90] *Epitome,* I, 313.

present, it is clearly manifested in the law.[91] Since this obligation of attendance is not stated with regard to titular bishops or other members of the clergy who are freely invited, it does not seem to exist.[92]

For these reasons it seems true to say that all those, and only those, who must under the law be invited to attend the provincial councils have in consequence the strict and corresponding obligation to attend them.

Article 4. Canonical Norms of Procedure

The rules given in the Code for conciliar procedure are few and clear. In accordance with canon 2, which affirms the force of liturgical laws in general,[93] the directions of the approved liturgical books,[94] which may be supplemented by helpful manuals,[95] govern the ceremonies of provincial councils. The present Article will not attempt to give a detailed exposition of the liturgical ceremonies, but rather to indicate the pertinent canonical principles.

A. Presiding at the Council

Canon 284: Metropolita, eoque legitime impedito vel sede archiepiscopali vacante, Suffraganeus antiquior promotione ad ecclesiam suffraganeam . . .

2°. Concilium convocat eique praeest.

[91] Canon 282, § 1: . . . assistere debent . . .; canon 282, § 2: . . . adesse debent . . .; canon 285: . . . intersint . . .; canon 286, § 1: . . . convenire debent . . .; canon 286, § 3: . . . mittant . . .; canon 286, § 4: . . . debentque invitati adesse . . .; canon 287, § 1: . . . interesse debent . . .; canon 289, § 1: . . . interesse debent . . .

[92] Titular bishops who receive an invitation to a *plenary* council are bound to attend, since this is explicitly stated in canon 282, § 2.

[93] Canon 2: . . . omnes liturgicae leges vim suam retinent, nisi earum aliqua in Codice expresse corrigatur.

[94] Cf. *Pontificale Romanum*, Vol. III, tit. 5, *Ordo ad Synodum; Caeremoniale Episcoporum*, Lib. I, cap. 31.

[95] Cf. Praxis Synodalis, *Manuale Synodi Dio[e]cesanae ac Provincialis Celebrandae* (ed. emendata, Neo-Eboraci, 1886) (hereafter cited as *Praxis Synodalis*); Moretti, III, nn. 2451-2502; *Baltimore Ceremonial*, pp. 376-390. Cf. Wernz-Vidal, II, 795, 796.

The metropolitan or, when the metropolitan is legitimately impeded, the senior suffragan bishop presides and opens the council.[96] At the beginning of the assembly, the profession of faith is prescribed.[97] This profession is made first by the general assembly, including the persons who have but a consultative vote, in the presence of the *praeses* or his delegate, and then by the presiding officer in the presence of the entire council.[98]

The law draws a sharp distinction between plenary and provincial councils with regard to the one who officially presides. Canon 288 clearly shows that at provincial councils the metropolitan is only a *primus inter pares*. He keeps order and directs the proceedings, but must always be guided by the will of the majority of his brother prelates.[99] It is not the discretionary option of the metropolitan or of the senior suffragan, but the majority vote of the council, that governs the manner of settlement and the issue of every question that may arise for decision: the matters to be treated at the council,[100] the order of business, the protracting of a session or of the number of sessions, the transfer [101] and close of the council,[102] the granting of an invitation and vote to titular bishops,[103] the judging

[96] Canon 284.

[97] Canon 1406, § 1. Canon 2403 states the penalty for a contumacious refusal to make the profession of faith.

[98] Canon 1406, § 1. Cf. Hanrahan, "The Law on Plenary Councils"—*The Clergy Review*, XIV (1938), 396; Wernz-Vidal, II, 682; Moretti, III, n. 2468.

[99] Cf. Sipos, *Enchiridion Iuris Canonici*, pp. 224, 225.

[100] Schemata of the proposed decrees are usually prepared and distributed among the Fathers in advance of the council. Cf. Wernz-Vidal, II, 682, 683. Decisions concerning the order of business, the matters to be treated, whether the vote is to be secret or open, etc., can be made at the first private congregation of the members whose right it is to exercise a deliberative vote. Cf. Scherer, *Handbuch des Kirchenrechtes*, I, 674; Augustine, *Commentary*, II, 305.

[101] For the transferring of a council Blat (*Commentarium*, II, 257) suggests as reasonable causes the arising of some emergency, such as interference with the liberty of the prelates, or the occurrence of an epidemic.

[102] Canon 288.

[103] Canon 286, § 2.

and accepting of an excuse for absence [104] or for a premature departure from the council,[105] the issuance of conciliar decrees [106] and the determination of the time and mode of their promulgation, dependent upon their previous review or revision by the Holy See.[107] It is the presiding officer, however, who has the personal responsibility for the sending of all the conciliar acts and decrees for the purpose of a proper review and official supervision on the part of the Sacred Congregation of the Council in Rome.[108]

B. Premature Departure

Canon 289. Concilio . . . provinciali inchoato, nemini eorum qui interesse debent, licet discedere, nisi iustam ob causam . . . a Concilii provincialis Patribus probatam.

Those who have the obligation of being present at the celebration of the provincial council, whether they possess a deliberative or a merely consultative vote, must remain until the council has formally adjourned. It would be derogatory to the solemnity and importance of the conciliar assembly, perhaps even to the successful completion of its business, if those whose presence is desired by the law could depart for arbitrary reasons.

Canon 289 resembles canon 225, which contains similar prescriptions for ecumenical councils. Canon 289 binds only those to whom an invitation for attendance at the council must be sent, since they alone have the obligation of attending the council.[109] Such persons may not depart from the council during the period of time intervening between the formal decree of opening at the first session and the final adjournment, unless they have presented a just excuse which has met with the approval of the majority of the Fathers.[110]

[104] Canon 287, § 1.

[105] Canon 289.

[106] Canon 290.

[107] Canon 291, § 1.

[108] Cf. canons 291, § 1; 304, § 2.

[109] Cf. *supra*, in the present Chapter, Article 3. Hence the norm of canon 289 does not apply to titular bishops who are freely invited.

[110] Cf. Blat, *Commentarium*, II, 258.

C. Precedence

The general norms of precedence[111] must be observed at provincial councils in the processions, in the order of seating and voting, and in the subscription of the decrees.[112]

1. Presiding Officer

The presiding officer precedes all others, even cardinals.[113] Since the metropolitan convokes the council and presides over it by law, he has a certain preeminence over the other members of the council.[114] One who has authority over others, whether it is derived from jurisdictional or merely dominative or domestic power, is granted by law precedence over those persons.[115]

2. Suffragan and Exempt Bishops

The precedence of suffragan bishops, since they are equal in rank (*gradus*) and sacred orders (*ordo*),[116] is determined by their seniority

[111] Cf., e. g., canons 106; 239, 21°; 269, § 2; 271; 280; 347; 450, § 2, 478; 491. Vermeersch-Creusen (*Epitome,* I, 202) and Michiels (*De Personis,* p. 561) indicate helpful and concise applications of the general norms of precedence. For outlines of the order of precedence in liturgical processions, cf. *Praxis Synodalis,* pp. 23, 24; Moretti, III, n. 2479. The Fathers of the council are empowered to settle controversies concerning precedence which may arise on the occasion of the conciliar proceedings. Cf. canon 106, 6°.

[112] *Caeremoniale Episcoporum,* Lib. I, cap. 31, n. 15; Cocchi, *Commentarium,* III, 135.

[113] Moretti, III, n. 2502. But at Mass a cardinal receives incensation before the metropolitan. Cf. *Caeremoniale Episcoporum,* Lib. I, cap. 23, nn. 27, 29.

[114] Canon 106, 2°: Cui est auctoritas in personas sive physicas sive morales, eidem ius est praecedentiae super illas. Cf. can. 6, I Council of Braga (561): "Item placuit ut conservato metropolitani episcopi primatu ceteri episcoporum secundum suae ordinationis tempus alius alio sedendi deferat locum."—Bruns, II, 34; c. 1, D. XVIII. Cf. Vermeersch-Creusen, *Epitome,* I, 202; Moretti, III, n. 2502.

[115] Cf. Beste, *Introductio in Codicem,* p. 163; cf. also canon 450, § 2, which grants a vicar forane precedence over the priests of his deanery.

[116] Cf. canon 106, 3°. *Gradus* denotes a preeminence, not of jurisdictional or dominative authority (cf. canon 106, 2°), but of title or rank, as, for instance,

according to the time of their preconization (made in the Consistory) or nomination (made outside the Consistory) to the episcopacy,[117] and not according to the time of their promotion to a suffragan see of the province.[118]

Exempt bishops follow the same rules of precedence as suffragan bishops.[119]

3. Titular Bishops

It is the opinion of Vermeersch-Creusen [120] that titular bishops, when they attend at the celebration of the council upon the free invitation of the Fathers, follow the same rules of precedence as suffragan bishops not only among themselves but also in relation

the rank of cardinal, of primate, of patriarch, or of titular archbishop. *Ordo* refers to the hierarchy of orders, including bishops, priests and ministers (cf. canon 108, § 3). Cf. Vermeersch-Creusen, *Epitome,* I, 201.

[117] Cf. S. R. C., *Iaren.,* 15 apr. 1904—*Decreta Authentica Congregationis Sacrorum Rituum* (5 vols., Romae: Ex Typographia Polyglotta, 1898-1901. Appendix I, 1912; Appendix II, 1927), n. 4133 (hereafter cited as *Decr. Auth. S. R. C.*); S. R. C., *Terulen.,* 20 nov. 1677—*Decr. Auth. S. R. C.,* n. 1606; S. R. C., *Segobricen.,* 21 mart. 1609—*Decr. Auth. S. R. C.,* n. 270. Cf. also "Annotationes"—*Periodica,* XIV (1925), 180-182, 180.

[118] Cf. Resp., Pontificia Commissio Interpretationis (hereafter cited as P. C. I.), 10 nov. 1925, ad II—*AAS,* XVII (1925), 582. As stated in canon 284, the convocation and presidency of the council, when the metropolitan is impeded, does not follow the usual order of precedence, since this twofold office devolves upon the bishop who is senior, not by promotion to the episcopal dignity, but by promotion to a suffragan see of the province. Cf. "Annotationes"—*Periodica,* XIV (1925), 181.

[119] Cf. Pallottini (*Collectio Omnium Conclusionum et Resolutionum Quae in Causis Propositis apud Sacram Congregationem Cardinalium S. Concilii Tridentini Interpretum Prodierunt ab eius Institutione Anno MCLXIV ad MDCCCLX, Distinctis Titulis Alphabetico Ordine per Materias Digesta* [18 vols., Romae, 1868-1895], XV, "Praecedentia," n. 86), who reports a decision of the S. C. C. (1596) to this effect. Vermeersch-Creusen (*Epitome,* I, p. 202, note 1) seem to consider titular bishops as being in the same category as exempt bishops, but this opinion appears to be at variance with a response of the S. C. C., which explicitly stated that a titular bishop who is freely invited to the council cannot be considered as an exempt bishop. Cf. S. C. C., *Aquen.,* 24 aug. 1850, ad III—*Fontes,* n. 4112.

[120] *Epitome,* I, 202, 313.

to the suffragan bishops. According to this opinion, titular bishops would not yield in precedence to those suffragan bishops whom they outrank according to the time of promotion to the episcopacy. The proponents of this opinion admit that a titular bishop may be subject to some particular suffragan bishop by reason of domicile or quasi-domicile, but they assert that the participation of titular bishops in the council is based, not on their domicile or quasi-domicile, but on their possession of the episcopacy, and that the only norm of precedence stated for bishops at councils is that which looks to seniority in the episcopal dignity.[121]

Neither the *Caeremoniale Episcoporum*[122] nor the reply given on November 10, 1935, by the Pontifical Commission for the Authentic Interpretation of the Code specifically mentions the precedence of titular bishops. On the contrary, the reply of the Pontifical Commission seems to exclude titular bishops, since it explicitly mentions only suffragan bishops.[123] Since residential bishops, and not titular bishops, are the ordinary members of councils, and since titular bishops, in a given case, may perhaps possess only a consultative vote,[124] there appears no indication that titular bishops are included under the term *episcopi* in the norms for precedence at the council, as stated in the *Caeremoniale Episcoporum*.[125] On the contrary,

[121] Cf. "Annotationes"—*Periodica,* XIV (1925), 181, 182; Vermeersch-Creusen, *Epitome,* I, p. 202, note I.

[122] Lib. I, cap. 31, n. 15.

[123] Resp., P. C. I., 10 nov. 1925, ad II: "Utrum vi canonis 106, 3°, praecedentia inter Episcopos *suffraganeos* [italics by the writer] in Concilio provinciali aliisque coetibus provincialibus definienda sit a die praeconizationis seu electionis ad episcopatum, an a die promotionis ad Ecclesiam suffraganeam?

"R.—Affirmative ad primam partem, negative ad secundam."—*AAS,* XVII (1925), 582.

[124] Cf. canon 286, § 2. Cf. also S. C. C., *Aquen.,* 24 aug. 1850, ad I—*Fontes,* n. 4112.

[125] Lib. I, cap. 31, n. 15: "In sessione vero, et ordine proferendi vota, observatum est, ut Episcopi praecedant iuxta ordinem eorum promotionis, nullo habito respectu ad dignitatem, vel praeeminentiam ecclesiarum. Dignitates, et Canonici Cathedralis Ecclesiae, cum capitulariter procedunt, aut sunt, praeferuntur ceteris omnibus; alias Abbates titulares, et habentes usum mitrae praecedunt, et post eos Commendatarii, deinde Dignitates, mox Procuratores Capitulorum Ecclesiarum Cathedralium, deinde ceteri pro cuiusque dignitate, et gradu, ut *cap. XXIII. § XIX. lib. 1, de ordine thurificandi* colligere licet."

it seems that the *Caeremoniale Episcoporum* prescinds from the question of the precedence of titular bishops, for a clear response of the Sacred Congregation of the Council stated that titular bishops do not precede suffragan bishops at provincial councils.[126] It appears, therefore, that titular bishops, since they enjoy a seat at the council only at the option of the Fathers, must yield in precedence to the suffragan bishops.[127]

4. Procurators

One who acts as procurator for another enjoys the precedence which is accorded to the person whom he represents; but procurators at councils and similar assemblies take their places after the attending bishops who are of the same rank as the principal of the proxy.[128] Therefore, the procurator of an absent titular archbishop follows all archbishops who are present, but precedes the residential bishops. The procurator of a residential bishop precedes the titular bishops, but follows the residential bishops.[129]

[126] S. C. C., *Aquen.*, 24 aug. 1850, ad. II: "Utrum [Episcopus mere titularis] praecedentia frui debeat quoad caeteros Episcopos Suffraganeos, si prius consecrationem episcopalem receperit?

"Ad II. Negative."—*Fontes*, n. 4112. Cf. canon 2.

[127] This opinion is supported by Wernz-Widal (II, 678), Prümmer (*Manuale Iuris Canonici* [3. ed. aucta et secundum recentissimas decisiones Romanas recognita, Friburgi Brisgoviae, 1922], p. 33) and Beste (*Introductio in Codicem*, p. 254).

[128] Canon 106, 1°. Cf. Woywod, *A Practical Commentary on the Code of Canon Law*, I, 47.

[129] Cf. Beste, *Introductio in Codicem*, p. 163.

CHAPTER VII

FORCE OF CONCILIAR DECREES

ARTICLE 1. PROMULGATION OF CONCILIAR DECREES

THE decrees which have been formulated and signed by the Fathers of the council do not have the force of law until a twofold requirement has been fulfilled: the decrees must receive the censorship and stand reviewed by the Holy See,[1] and subsequent thereto they must be promulgated.

Promulgation may be defined as the authentic publication of a law made to a community.[2] Since a law is not merely a plan or a norm which exists solely in the mind of the legislator, but a rule of action for the community, it must be manifested to the community by the authority of him who has the power to impose such rule of activity. It is the public manifestation of the legislator's will to the community that induces the juridic efficacy of a law.[3] It would not suffice for the legislator to intimate his will merely to certain individuals, since a law is intended, not for just a few individuals, but for the community as such.[4]

Moreover, the intimation of the law to the community at large must be made authentically, that is, the publication of the law must be made by the authority of the lawgiver himself or by another with the authentic mandate of the legislator.[5] The absolute necessity of the promulgation of laws is certain both from the very nature of a law and from the clear principle enunciated in canon 8, § 1: *Leges instituuntur, cum promulgantur.* Van Hove [6] paraphrases this canon with the statement that there is no law and therefore no obligation before a law is promulgated.

[1] Cf. *supra*, pp. 48-52.

[2] Michiels, *Normae Generales*, I, 151; Van Hove, *De Legibus*, p. 112.

[3] Michiels, *ibid.*, p. 149.

[4] Benedictus XIV, *De Syn.*, Lib. XIII, cap. 4, n. 1; Van Hove, *De Legibus*, p. 114.

[5] Michiels, *Normae Generales*, I, 149.

[6] *De Legibus*, p. 115.

Since the legislator in the provincial council is not the metropolitan alone but the Fathers as a body, the majority vote of the Fathers will determine the time and mode of promulgation, which promulgation will take place, of course, only after the Holy See's revision of the decrees.[7] It seems that the specification of the period of time during which the promulgated law will not as yet operate with binding force (the *vacatio legis,* if one is to be granted) and of the mode in which the promulgation is to be made should be clearly expressed in the acts or decrees of the council.[8] The Fathers may authorize the metropolitan alone to promulgate the decrees in the manner which they have determined[9] or they may promulgate the decrees jointly.[10]

In contrast to canon 335, § 2, which states that diocesan statutes begin to bind immediately upon promulgation, unless they contain a contrary provision, the present canon seems to manifest the implicit desire of the lawmaker that a certain interval of grace and favor from the law intervene as designated in the decree of promul-

[7] Canon 291, § 1.

[8] Cf. the following footnote for a clear example.

[9] Cf. Chelodi, *Ius de Personis,* p. 396; Cocchi, *Commentarium,* III, 136. Cf. decree of promulgation, II Council of Toronto (1938): "Nos, Metropolita et Suffraganei Episcopi, huius Provinciae Torontinae Ordinarii, omnia et singula, quae in hoc Concilio Provinciali decreta et sancita sunt, pro necessitatibus Ecclesiae et salute animarum nostris in dioecesibus, filiali reverentia et obsequentissimo animo Apostolicae Sedi submittimus. Quia vero nulla lex vim obligandi habere potest nisi promulgetur, statuimus, ut postquam a Sancta Sede decreta huius Concilii expensa et recognita fuerint, quamprimum promulgentur.

"Ne autem ullus supersit dubitandi locus de tempore, quo incipiet obligatio suscipiendi et exsequendi decreta huius Concilii Provincialis Torontini Secundi, declaramus et omnibus notum facimus cuncta et singula, quae in hoc Concilio decreta et constituta sunt, vim suam habere plenariosque et integros effectus sortiri per universas huius Provinciae ecclesias, tribus mensibus a die qui ab Ordinario Torontino apponetur editioni typis impressae eorundem Decretorum, in nomine Patris et Filii et Spiritus Sancti."—*Acta et Decreta Concilii Provincialis Torontini Secundi, Toronti in Ecclesia Metropolitana Celebrati Diebus XIII, XIV, XV Decembris MCMXXXVIII* (Toronto: [?], 1940), p. 83.

[10] Cf. *Acta et Decreta Concilii Provincialis Portlandensis in Oregon Quarti* (1932), p. 11.

gation.[11] A period of inoperativeness on the part of the newly promulgated law appears to be fitting, since the decrees will have force in a large territory, but the decision rests with the judgment of the Fathers.[12]

As early as the year 693 it was prescribed that diocesan synods be held within six months after the conclusion of the provincial councils. The purpose to be served was the publication of the conciliar decrees with a view to securing their due observance.[13] In the year 1215 it was ordered that diocesan synods be celebrated annually for this purpose.[14] The Council of Trent (1545-1563) renewed the legislation regarding the annual celebration of diocesan synods,[15] but it did not specifically assign to them the task of publishing the provincial decrees.

Examples of promulgation outside diocesan synods [16] furnish the

[11] Canon 291, § 2: . . . ipsimet autem Concilii Patres designent et modum promulgationis decretorum et *tempus quo* decreta promulgata obligare incipiant. (Italics are the writer's.) Cf. Michiels, *Normae Generales,* I, 243.

[12] Laws of the Holy See which are published in the *Acta Apostolicae Sedis* begin to bind only three months after the day of publication, unless other provision be expressly made (canon 9). An interval of four and a half months was provided by the IV Provincial Council of Portland (1932): *Acta et Decreta Concilii Provincialis Portlandensis in Oregon Quarti,* p. 11; one of three months was provided by the II Provincial Council of Toronto (1938): *Acta et Decreta Concilii Provincialis Torontini Secundi,* p. 83; one of two months was provided by the Provincial Council of Revenna (1855): Can. 10, § II—*Coll. Lac.,* VI, 211, d.

[13] Can. 7, XVI Council of Toledo (693): ". . . unusquisque episcoporum admonitionibus suis infra sex mensium spatia . . . cunctam dioecesis suae plebem aggregare nequaquam moretur, quatenus coram eis publice omnia reserata de his, quae eodem anno in concilio acta vel definita extiterint, plenissime notiores efficiantur . . ."—Bruns, I, 372.

[14] Can. 6, IV Council of the Lateran (1215): ". . . et quae statuerint [in Conciliis provincialibus] faciant observari, publicaturi ea in episcopalibus synodis annuatim per singulas dioeceses celebrandis."—Mansi, XXII, 991.

[15] Sess. XXIV, *de ref.,* c. 2.

[16] Cf. can. 10, § II, Provincial Council of Ravenna (1855)—*Coll. Lac.,* VI, 211, d (promulgation by attaching the decrees to the doors of the metropolitan and other churches); promulgation by the metropolitan (1862) after the Council of Urbino (1859)—*Coll. Lac.,* VI, 1; can. 13, III Provincial Council of Quebec (1863)—*Coll. Lac.,* III, 679, a, b (promulgation by the comprovincial bishops

clue that the publication of the provincial decrees in diocesan synods was sometimes a divulgation rather than a promulgation of the conciliar law.[17] The distinction between divulgation and promulgation appears clearly in the teaching of Suarez (1548-1617).[18] This distinction underlies the very basis of a reply given by the Sacred Congregation of the Holy Office on September 10, 1896. In this reply it was intimated that the publication of the provincial decrees by the diocesan synods was not required for the promulgation of the conciliar law.[19]

Promulgation is the first authentic pronouncement of the law to the community as such and establishes the objective obligation of the law. The subsequent divulgation through preaching, in the press, or by means of other agencies, spreads the knowledge of the law to its subjects and removes from them all excuse for subjective ignorance regarding their obligation.[20] The celebration of diocesan synods will of course continue to offer a most effective means for spreading the knowledge and ensuring the observance of provincial laws after their promulgation.[21]

within or outside diocesan synods); promulgation by the metropolitan (1863) after the V Provincial Council of Prague (1860)—*Coll. Lac.*, V, 410; promulgation by the apostolic legate (1868) after the II Plenary Council of Baltimore (1866)—*Coll. Lac.*, III, 323-326.

17 Cocchi (*Commentarium*, III, 136) does not consider the distinction between promulgation and divulgation in his general statement that before the Code the promulgation of provincial decrees was prescribed through diocesan synods to be held within six months after the completion of the provincial council.

18 *De Legibus*, Lib. III, cap. 16, n. 3.

19 S. C. S. Off., 10 sept. 1896, ad 2: "Utrum decreta Conciliorum sive plenariorum sive provincialium a S. Sede *in forma communi sive specifica confirmata, vel adprobata, vel saltem recognita* omnimoda vi careant, nisi in statuta dioecesana iam fuerint incorporata, et quidem tantum valeant, in quantum sic fuerint incorporata.

"Ad 2. Negative—Ssmus adprobavit."—*Fontes*, n. 1184.

20 Cf. Michiels, *Normae Generales*, I, 151, 152.

21 De Meester, II, 117: "Concilium provinciale cum maxima utilitate subsequetur Synodi dioecesanae celebratio ad meliorem divulgationem et applicationem eorum quae in provinciali Concilio acta et decisa fuere."

Article 2. Interpretation of Conciliar Decrees

The interpretation of law is commonly divided into three categories, namely, private, customary and authentic interpretation.[22] Private interpretation is that which is given by the private authority of a teacher, and thus may be either accepted or rejected by others, since in and of itself it does not bind others, inasmuch as its whole force lies in the correctness of its reasoning and in the application of a skilled jurisprudence. Customary interpretation is that which is derived from the constant practice of the people in the observance of the law.[23] Authentic interpretation, which alone is considered here, is that which proceeds officially from a person in authority, so that it binds the subject to whom it is directed, namely, the whole community if the interpretation is given in the form of a legal enactment, or individual persons if the interpretation is given in the form of a judicial sentence or of a particular rescript.[24]

It seems clear that a provincial council can authentically interpret the decrees of a previous provincial council, since it has the power to make laws and is the legitimate successor of the preceding councils.[25] But, can individual bishops, even without delegation, authentically interpret provincial decrees?

Toso [26] affirms that they can do so, either singly or collectively. Michiels [27] makes a distinction. He denies that the power of authentic interpretation belongs to local ordinaries on their own authority, since conciliar laws are not properly of their own, but of a superior authority, namely, of the council as such. However, he concedes the power of authentic interpretation to the individual bishops for their own dioceses on the grounds that they have the power to dispense from the provincial laws. He regards the lesser

[22] Cf. Van Hove, *De Legibus*, p. 251.

[23] Canon 29: Consuetudo est optima legum interpres.

[24] Cf. Van Hove, *loc. cit.*; canon 17, §§ 2, 3.

[25] Canon 17, § 1: Leges authentice interpretatur legislator eiusve successor . . .

[26] *Commentaria Minora*, I, 56.

[27] *Normae Generales*, I, p. 397, note 1.

power of authentically interpreting the law as an element that is contained in the greater power to dispense from the law.[28]

However, Van Hove [29] aptly shows that the power to dispense, as conceded in canon 291, § 2, applies only to particular cases, and therefore does not extend to an interpretation made in the form of a legal enactment. It may be granted that the power of authentically interpreting the law belongs to the bishop for an individual case only, since it is contained in his power to apply the law by means of a judicial sentence [30] and in his power to grant a particular rescript.[31] But, since the legislative jurisdiction of individual bishops does not extend to the enactments of provincial councils, an individual bishop does not intrinsically possess the power to issue an authentic interpretation by way of a legal enactment.[32]

The delegation of the power to interpret provincial laws is another question. Wernz-Vidal,[33] Maroto,[34] and Michiels [35] affirm that the council can delegate the power of authentic interpretation either to the metropolitan alone or to the members of the council collectively.[36] This view is supported by the practice of provincial

[28] Michiels, *loc. cit.*: "De facto tamen illa potestate [authentice interpretandi leges conciliares] fruuntur pro sua diocesi, vi can. 291, § 2; potestas enim in iis dispensandi, qua aliquid majus, necessario comprehendit potestatem interpretandi, qua aliquid minus, juxta R. J. 35 in VI°."

[29] *De Legibus*, p. 253, note 4.

[30] Schmidt, *The Principles of Authentic Interpretation in Canon 17 of the Code of Canon Law*, The Catholic University of America Canon Law Studies, n. 141 (Washington, D. C.: The Catholic University of America Press, 1941), p. 50; Wernz, I, n. 130.

[31] Van Hove, *loc. cit.* Cf. canons 291, § 2; 15.

[32] Schmidt, *loc. cit.* Hence the opinion of Bouix (*De Concilio Provinciali*, p. 91) that the metropolitan, as the first authority in the province, has the inherent power to interpret provincial laws, appears to lack a foundation.

[33] *Ius Canonicum*, II, 684, 685.

[34] *Inst.*, I, 251.

[35] *Normae Generales*, I, 397. Bouix (1808-1870) taught the same doctrine in his work, *De Concilio Provinciali*, p. 91.

[36] Authors have not considered the question whether the bishops could be delegated to give in their own dioceses individual and independent authentic interpretations of the provincial laws. Such a measure would not seem feasible, since there should be not more than one source of authentic interpretation of provincial law within the province.

councils,[37] and accords with canon 17, § 1, which states that the power of authentic interpretation can be delegated by the legislator.[38]

However, Van Hove [39] denies that the power of authentic interpretation can be committed either to the metropolitan or to the bishops of the province as a group, apart from the exercise of such power of interpretation by the council itself in its actual sessions. He argues that the legislative power of a provincial council is limited to the actual time of the celebration of the council. In reply it may be said that the laws of a provincial council continue to exercise their force after the close of the council, and it is only the enacting of new laws that would require the celebration of a new council. If, therefore, the council delegated its power to interpret laws, this delegation would seem to continue in force after the close of the council.[40]

But, as stated by Van Hove,[41] the issuance of an authentic interpretation of a truly doubtful law, or the issuance of an extensive or restrictive interpretation as equivalent to a new provincial law, would necessitate all the formalities prescribed in the celebration of a provincial council, including the official revision of the interpretative law by the Holy See.[42] On the other hand, for the issuance of a

[37] Cf. can. 10, § VIII, Provincial Council of Ravenna (1855): "Si de eorundem sensu ullum unquam exortum fuerit prudens dubinum et difficultas, ejus et omnium, quae decretis praefatis continentur, declarationem, interpretationem et explicationem Nobis vel Metropolitano pro tempore reservamus, usque dum alia provincialis Synodus in Ravennatensi provincia habeatur, salva tamen semper Sedis Apostolicae auctoritate."—*Coll. Lac.*, VI, 212, c. Cf. also Provincial Council of Tours (1849)—*Coll. Lac.*, IV, 258, c; Provincial Council of Vienna (1858)—*Coll. Lac.*, V, 152, d, 153; Provincial Council of Kalocsa (1860)—*Coll. Lac.*, V, 335, b; Provincial Council of Prague (1860)—*Coll. Lac.*, V, 401, d; Provincial Council of Utrecht (1865)—*Coll. Lac.*, V, 784, a; Can. 4, Provincial Council of New Granada (1868)—*Coll. Lac.*, VI, 473, d; Wernz, I, n. 130, note 184.

[38] Cf. Ojetti, *Commentarium in Codicem Iuris Canonici*, I, 135; Toso, *Commentaria Minora*, I, 54.

[39] *De Legibus*, p. 253.

[40] Cf. canon 207, § 1: Potestas delegata exstinguitur . . . non autem resoluto iure delegantis, nisi in duobus casibus de quibus in can. 61.

[41] *De Legibus*, p. 253.

[42] Cf. canons 17, § 2; 291, § 1.

merely declarative interpretation of a law no promulgation is required.[43] Hence it seems that the metropolitan or the bishops as a group can be delegated by the council to give interpretations of the provincial decrees whenever the interpretations are of a merely declarative character. A declarative interpretation of law ". . . explains what is already present; it needs no promulgation; it is retroactive, leaving aside the material object of its activity. . . The Code understands this species of interpretation only of law which is already clear in itself and which could have been known before the interpretation appeared . . ." [44]

But what course is to be followed if there should arise a true *dubium iuris*, a serious difficulty of interpretation, concerning a provincial law? Van Hove [45] remarks that in such a case the local ordinary is free to issue a diocesan statute, as a law *"praeter legem concilii"* (but not as an authentic interpretation of the conciliar law). The settlement by authentic interpretation of a true *dubium iuris* concerning a provincial decree may be referred to the Holy See, as the supreme legislator,[46] to a plenary council, or to the subsequent provincial council.[47]

Article 3. Dispensation from Conciliar Decrees

Canon 291, § 2. Decreta Concilii . . . provincialis promulgata obligant in suo cuiusque territorio universo, nec Ordinarii locorum ab iisdem dispensare possunt, nisi in casibus particularibus et iusta de causa.

[43] Cf. canon 17, § 2.

[44] Schmidt, *The Principles of Authentic Interpretation in Canon 17 of the Code of Canon Law*, p. 174.

[45] *De Legibus*, p. 253.

[46] Cf. canon 17, § 1. On August 2, 1918, the Sacred Consistorial Congregation declared that the enactments of the provincial councils of Westminster remained still in force for the whole territory, although the province of Westminster had been dismembered (cf. canon 1421)—*AAS*, X (1918), 365.

[47] Cf. canon 17, § 1.

A dispensation is a relaxation from the law in a special case.[48] Michiels [49] explains that a "special case" is not distinguished from a "particular case" which latter expression was the one commonly used in the definition current before the Code. This point is of special interest in connection with the canon under consideration, for it contains the phrase, *in casibus particularibus*. It is of the nature of a dispensation to remove the obligation of a law for certain persons (physical or moral), things or circumstances, while the law itself does not suffer abrogation or derogation, but remains intact, not only so far as other subjects of the community are concerned, but even as regards the person dispensed, in cases and circumstances other than those for which he was dispensed.[50] However, the restriction relative to the granting of a dispensation in a special or in a particular case does not imply that the dispensation cannot be granted with a view to exempting subjects from a law of recurring obligation, such as that of the Divine Office,[51] or for the purpose of favoring a whole community, a parish or a diocese, provided that only a temporary relaxation of the law be in question.[52]

The power to dispense is proper to the lawmaker, to his successor or to the superior of each of these. Any of these three can in turn authorize a delegate with the use of the same power.[53] Only the legislator or one who shares his power can release from the bond

[48] Canon 80.

[49] *Normae Generales,* II, 454.

[50] Michiels, *loc. cit.*

[51] The granting of a perpetual exemption from the recitation of the Divine Office would constitute a *privilegium contra ius* rather than a dispensation. Cf. D'Annibale, *Summula Theologiae Moralis* (3 vols., 5. ed. diligenter revisa et novissimis SS. Congregationum decretis locupletata, Romae, 1908), I, 220.

[52] Maroto, *Inst.,* I, 361: "Casus specialis in dispensatione haberi potest vel quia conceditur alicui personae particulari tam physicae quam morali, vel quia conceditur toti communitati perfectae pro uno actu vel pro certo tempore. Effectus igitur dispensationis est auferre vel suspendere obligationem legis *in casibus particularibus.*" (Italics are the writer's.) Cf. Reilly, *The General Norms of Dispensation,* p. 1; Michiels, *Normae Generales,* II, 454; Beste, *Introductio in Codicem,* p. 126; cf. also canon 1245, § 2, as a specific example.

[53] Canon 80.

of the law. The granting of a dispensation is thus an act of jurisdiction.[54] Anyone who receives delegated dispensatory power can dispense validly only within the limits of his mandate.[55]

It is clear that the laws of the provincial council, which are binding throughout the entire territory subject to the council, emanate from a higher jurisdiction than that possessed by the individual members of the council. The legislator at a provincial council is not an individual bishop, but the council as such, and hence the individual bishop inherently lacks the power to dispense from the conciliar decrees.[56] Therefore, canon 291, § 2, does not involve a restriction of the local ordinary's power; rather it bespeaks a positive concession of dispensatory power as deriving from the law of the Code.[57] By the law of the Code, then, there is conferred upon bishops and other local ordinaries the power to dispense from the provincial conciliar laws upon two conditions: (1) in particular cases only, and (2) for a just cause. If either condition were lacking, the granting of the dispensation would be not only illicit but also invalid in view of the absence of all operative dispensatory power.[58]

Among the local ordinaries authorized to grant dispensations from the provincial conciliar laws are included the diocesan vicars general.[59] The dispensing power which through canon 291, § 2, is granted to local ordinaries exists as an ordinary power. Those who possess this power can accordingly delegate it to others.[60] A comparison of canon 291, § 2, with canon 81 indicates moreover that, so far as the generality of laws is concerned, local ordinaries have wider powers for dispensing from provincial laws than for dispensing from the laws of the Code.[61]

[54] Maroto, *loc. cit.*

[55] Cf. canon 203, § 1.

[56] Cf. Suarez, *De Legibus*, Lib. VI, cap. 15, n. 4; Benedictus XIV, *De Syn.*, Lib. XIII, cap. 5, n. 8.

[57] Reilly, *The General Norms of Dispensation*, p. 89.

[58] Cf. canon 84, § 1; Toso, *Commentaria Minora*, III, 111.

[59] Cf. canons 368, § 1; 198.

[60] Cf. canon 199, § 1; Beste, *Introductio in Codicem*, p. 255.

[61] Canon 81 states that the local ordinary can dispense from the common law only if an urgent matter arises in which the peril of grave loss or harm

A just cause is required for the validity of all dispensations which are granted by an inferior from the law of his superior.[62] If the legislator himself were to dispense from his law without a cause, he would act illicitly by showing favoritism to one or more of his subjects, but he would dispense validly for the simple reason that the whole obligation of the law depends upon his will.[63]

Again, the legislator himself could grant a general dispensation even for an indefinite period, since he has the power to abrogate his law. But since local ordinaries individually lack competency over provincial laws, they can grant a territorial dispensation only for a temporary period and upon the *conditio sine qua non,* for validity, of an existing justifying cause. The council itself, however, has full dispensing powers over its own laws, and hence in virtue of canon 199, § 1, could widen the dispensatory powers conceded in canon 291, § 2.[64]

Unless he has received express delegation, the local ordinary can dispense only those who are in some way his subjects,[65] including persons without a settled home (*vagi*) and travelers (*peregrini*) [66] who are present within his territory, but he can dispense anywhere in the world those who are his personal subjects by reason of a domicile or a quasi-domicile,[67] since the granting of a dispensation is an act of voluntary (non-judicial) jurisdiction.[68]

What constitutes the just cause which is required for a dispensation? This question cannot be answered absolutely, since the circumstances of places and persons must be weighed in proportion

is threatened, with the two added conditions that recourse to the Holy See is difficult, and the dispensation is one which is usually granted by the Holy See.

[62] Canon 84, § 1. Cf. Ojetti, *Commentarium in Codicem Iuris Canonici,* I, 334; Maroto, *Inst.,* I, 365.

[63] Maroto, *loc. cit.*

[64] Reilly, *The General Norms of Dispensation,* p. 90; Michiels, *Normae Generales,* II, 489.

[65] Cf. canons 291, § 2, and 82.

[66] Cf. canons 91 and 14. Cf. also Wernz-Vidal, I, 472.

[67] Cf. canon 94, § 1.

[68] Cf. canon 201, § 3. Cf. also D'Annibale, *Summula Theologiae Moralis,* I, 222, and canon 1245, § 1.

to the varying gravity of the different laws.[69] Hence it is left to the prudent judgment of the grantor of the dispensation to determine whether it is reasonable and equitable to remove the obligation of the law in a given instance.[70] But it is certain that the cause need not be so weighty that it would of itself excuse from the observance of the law, since in that case a dispensation would not be required at all.[71]

A just cause may be stated to exist ". . . if in view of the particular circumstances the observance of the law would (1) constitute a proportionately grave difficulty beyond the inconvenience commonly experienced in abiding by a law, or (2) impede some reasonably proportionate benefit which would result from the relaxation of the law." [72] In case of a doubt concerning the sufficiency of the cause presented for a dispensation, the dispensation can be granted both licitly and validly.[73]

[69] Cf. Michiels, *Normae Generales,* II, 506, 507, for an enumeration of the varying grades of causes for dispensation as required in different parts of the Code.

[70] Cf. Maroto, *Inst.,* I, 365: "Sufficit ea causa, quae omnibus circumstantiis legis et personae consideratis, dignoscitur rationi conveniens, ita ut ex dispensatione concessa bonum commune non laedatur et bonum personae dispensatae augeatur." Cf. Guiniven, *The Precept of Hearing Mass,* The Catholic University of America Canon Law Studies, n. 158 (Washington, D. C.: The Catholic University of America Press, 1942), pp. 161, 162.

[71] Reilly, *The General Norms of Dispensation,* p. 107; Vermeersch-Creusen, *Epitome,* I, 170.

[72] Reilly, *ibid.,* p. 108.

[73] Canon 84, § 2. Cf. Reilly, *ibid.,* p. 113.

CONCLUSIONS

1. The *ferendae sententiae* sanction of suspension from office (with the added penalty between the years 1215 and 1234 of suspension from benefice) for failure to convoke or to attend provincial councils, which sanction prevailed from the year 1215 until the time of the present Code of Canon Law, is no longer in effect. (Pp. 12-14, 75.)

2. Provincial decrees revoke contrary diocesan statutes, unless there be express provision to the contrary. (Pp. 31, 32.)

3. It would be rash to assert that less than three members who have the right of a deliberative vote can constitute a provincial council without the authorization of the Holy See; but there appears no compelling proof that more than three members are required as a condition for validity. (Pp. 32-42.)

4. Decisions of provincial councils are determined by a majority of the deliberative votes. (Pp. 42, 43.)

5. The review and revision accorded by the Holy See do not constitute an official act that sanates or changes the intrinsic nature of conciliar decrees, but this official act is required for their licit and valid promulgation. (Pp. 48-52.)

6. The Code stresses the function of provincial councils in promoting "one and the same ecclesiastical discipline." Rapid and facile modes of modern transportation accentuate the need for a uniform ecclesiastical discipline, which is closely connected with the progress of faith and morality, inasmuch as it forestalls the emergence of scandal, lends aid in the combating of errors and abuses, and promotes the vigorous observance of the common law. (Pp. 53-72.)

7. Bishops and others who share the privileges of canon 1557, § 1, are exempt from conciliar penal sanctions. (Pp. 69-71.)

8. The culpable failure to convoke a provincial council may be attributed to the senior suffragan bishop only when the metropolitan is legitimately impeded or when the metropolitan see is vacant. The culpable neglect of the metropolitan in this matter does not confer a devolved right or obligation upon the senior suffragan. (Pp. 73-79.)

9. Canon 304, § 2, states an exception to canon 283. (Pp. 79-81.)

10. The convocation of provincial councils oftener than once in twenty years requires the consent of the majority of the conciliar members. (P. 85.)

11. According to the more common interpretation of canon 105, it is required for the valid selection of the place for the celebration of the provincial council that the metropolitan consult the conciliar members as a group. (Pp. 85-89.)

12. Members of provincial councils who enjoy the right of a deliberative vote granted to them by the law are the following:

(1) Local ordinaries (from the time when they have taken canonical possession of their office), not excluding those who exercise full powers of administration *sede impedita,* but excluding vicars general. (Pp. 90-98.)

(2) Procurators if they are coadjutor or auxiliary bishops to the bishops whom they represent at the council. (Pp. 98, 99.)

Members of provincial councils who enjoy the right of a deliberative vote accorded to them by authority are the titular bishops who as residents of the province have received an invitation to attend the council, the invitation being extended as a result of the majority consent of the members who take part in the council with a deliberative vote. The extended invitation implies for these titular bishops the right to exercise a deliberative vote, unless the council rules otherwise. (P. 99.)

All other persons invited to provincial councils have a merely consultative vote.

13. Only those relative to whom the law states an unconditional requirement that they be invited are bound by the obligation of attending provincial councils. (Pp. 106-109.)

14. Suffragan and exempt bishops take precedence according to the time of their preconization or nomination to the episcopacy. They precede the titular bishops, not only when the latter have a merely consultative vote, but also when they enjoy a deliberative vote, at the option of the council. (Pp. 112-115.)

15. The acts or decrees of provincial councils should contain an express provision regarding the time and the mode for the promulga-

tion of the decrees. The setting of an interval of time during which the promulgated law awaits its ultimate operative efficacy is not strictly mandatory, but ordinarily proves desirable. (Pp. 117, 118.)

16. Conciliar delegation of the power of authentic interpretation to the metropolitan or to the members of the council collectively is restricted to the merely declarative interpretations of the provincial decrees. Only the provincial council itself or a higher authority can by means of an authentic interpretation resolve a true *dubium iuris* concerning the provincial decrees. (Pp. 121-123.)

17. Bishops and vicars general can dispense by ordinary power from provincial decrees, according to the norms of canon 291, § 2. They can validly grant a territorial dispensation, but only for a temporary period and provided that there exists a just cause for the dispensation. (Pp. 123-127.)

BIBLIOGRAPHY

Sources

Acta Apostolicae Sedis, Commentarium Officiale, Romae, 1909 —.

Acta et Decreta Concilii Provincialis Portlandensis in Oregon Quarti, Portlandiae in Ecclesia Metropolitana Celebrati, Diebus VIII, IX, X Septembris MCMXXXII, Portland: Sentinel Printery, 1934.

Acta et Decreta Concilii Provincialis Torontini Secundi, Toronti in Ecclesia Metropolitana Celebrati Diebus XIII, XIV, XV Decembris MCMXXXVIII, Toronto: [?], 1940.

Acta et Decreta Sacrorum Conciliorum Recentiorum, Collectio Lacensis 7 vols., auctoribus G. Schneemann (Vols. I-VI), et T. Granderath (Vol. VII), Friburgi Brisgoviae, 1870-1890.

Bouscaren, T. Lincoln, *The Canon Law Digest,* 2 vols., Milwaukee: Bruce, 1934-1943.

Bruns, H. T., *Canones Apostolorum et Conciliorum Saeculorum IV-VII,* 2 vols., Berolini, 1839.

Bullarum Diplomatum et Privilegiorum Sanctorum Romanorum Pontificum Taurinensis Editio, 24 vols. in 25, 1857-1883, Vol. VIII, Neapoli, 1883.

Caeremoniale Episcoporum, ed. typica, Ratisbonae, Neo Eboraci et Cincinnatii, 1886.

Ceremonial for the Use of the Catholic Churches in the United States of America, 8. ed. revised, Philadelphia, 1894.

Codex Iuris Canonici Pii X Pontificis Maximi iussu digestus Benedicti XV auctoritate promulgatus, Romae: Typis Polyglottis Vaticanis, 1917.

Codicis Iuris Canonici Fontes, cura Emi Petri Card. Gasparri editi, 9 vols., Romae: Typis Polyglottis Vaticanis, 1923-1939 (Vols. VII-IX, ed. cura et studio Emi Iustiniani Card. Serédi).

Collectanea S. Congregationis de Propaganda Fide, 2 vols., Romae: Typographia Polyglotta de Propaganda Fide, 1907.

Corpus Iuris Canonici, ed. Lipsiensis 2. post Aemilii Ludovici Richteri curas . . . instruxit Aemilius Friedberg, 2 vols., Lipsiae: Tauchnitz, 1879-1881; ed. anastatice repetita, Lipsiae: Tauchnitz, 1928.

Corpus Iuris Civilis, 3 vols., Berolini: Apud Weidmannos, 1928-1929; Vol. I, 15. ed., *Institutiones,* recognovit P. Krueger; *Digesta,* recognovit Th. Mommsen, retractavit P. Krueger; Vol. II, *Codex Iustinianus,* 10. ed., recognovit et retractavit P. Krueger; Vol. III, *Novellae,* 5. ed., recognovit R. Schoell, opus Schoellii morte interceptum absolvit G. Kroll.

Decreta Authentica Congregationis Sacrorum Rituum, 5 vols., Romae: Ex Typographia Polyglotta, 1898-1901. Appendix I, 1912; Appendix II, 1927.

Decretum Gratiani emendatum et notationibus illustratum, una cum glossis, Gregorii XIII Pont. Max. iussu editum, 2 vols., Romae, 1582.

Gams, Pius, *Series Episcoporum Ecclesiae Catholicae,* 2 vols. in 1, Ratisbonae, 1873-1886.

Haddan, A. W.-Stubbs, W., *Councils and Ecclesiastical Documents Relating to Great Britain and Ireland,* 3 vols. in 4, Oxford, 1869-1878.

Hardouin, J., *Acta Conciliorum et Epistolae Decretales,* 12 vols., Parisiis, 1714-1715.

Jaffé, Philippus, *Regesta Pontificum Romanorum ab condita Ecclesia ad annum post Christum natum MCXCVIII,* 2. ed., correctam et auctam auspiciis Gulielmi Wattenbach curaverunt S. Loewenfeld, F. Kaltenbrunner, P. Ewald, 2 vols. in 1, Lipsiae, 1885-1888.

Mansi, Ioannes, *Sacrorum Conciliorum Nova et Amplissima Collectio,* 53 vols. in 60, Paris, Arnhem, Leipzig, 1901-1927.

Monumenta Germaniae Historica, Gregorii I Papae Registrum Epistolarum, 4 vols., ed. L. M. Hartmann et P. Ewald, *Epistolarum,* Vol. I, pars II, Berolini, 1891.

Monumenta Germaniae Historica, Legum Sectio III, Concilia, 2 vols. in 4, ed. F. Maassen, A. Werminghoff, H. Bastgen, Hannoverae et Lipsiae, 1893-1924.

Official Catholic Directory, The, 4 parts, Part IV, *The Catholic Church in Ireland, England, Scotland, Wales, Cuba and Mexico,* New York: Kenedy, 1946.

Pallottini, Salvator, *Collectio Omnium Conclusionum et Resolutionum Quae in Causis Propositis apud Sacram Congregationem Cardinalium S. Concilii Tridentini Interpretum Prodierunt ab eius Institutione Anno MCLXIV ad MDCCCLX, Distinctis Titulis Alphabetico Ordine per Materias Digesta,* 18 vols., Romae, 1868-1895.

Pontificale Romanum, 3 vols., nova ed., Parisiis, 1850-1852.

Potthast, Augustus, *Regesta Pontificum Romanorum inde ab anno post Christum natum MCXCVIII ad annum MCCCIV,* 2 vols., Berolini, 1874-1875.

Praxis Synodalis, Manuale Synodi Dio[e]cesanae ac Provincialis Celebrandae, ed. emendata, Neo-Eboraci, 1886.

Sartori, Cosmas, *Enchiridion Canonicum,* 3. ed., emendata et aucta (1917-1932), Hankow: Missio Catholica, 1932.

Thiel, Andreas, *Epistolae Romanorum Pontificum Genuinae et Quae ad Eos Scriptae Sunt a S. Hilario usque ad Pelagium II,* Vol. I, Brunsbergae, 1868.

Turner, Cuthbertus, *Ecclesiae Occidentalis Monumenta Iuris Antiquissima, Canonum et Conciliorum Graecorum Interpretationes Latinae,* 2 vols. in 6, Oxonii: E. Typographia Clarendoniana, Vol. II, pars II, 1913.

Authors

André, Michel, *Cours Alphabétique et Méthodique de Droit Canon,* 2 vols. in 4, Paris, 1844.

Augustine, Charles, *A Commentary on the New Code of Canon Law,* 8 vols., Vol. II, St. Louis, 1918; Vol. VI, 2. ed., 1923.

Ayrinhac, H., *Administrative Legislation in the New Code of Canon Law*, New York: Longmans, Green, 1930.

Bargilliat, M., *Praelectiones Juris Canonici*, 28. ed. ab auctore recognita et recentioribus decretis accommodata, 2 vols., Parisiis, 1913.

Baronius, Caesar, *Annales Ecclesiastici*, ed. A. Theiner, 37 vols., Vols. I-XXVIII, Barri-Ducis, 1864-1875; Vols. XXIX-XXXVII, Parisiis, 1876-1883.

Barrett, John, *A Comparative Study of the Councils of Baltimore and the Code of Canon Law*, The Catholic University of America Canon Law Studies, n. 83, Washington, D. C.: The Catholic University of America, 1932.

Bastnagel, Clement, *The Appointment of Parochial Adjuvants and Assistants*, The Catholic University of America Canon Law Studies, n. 58, Washington, D. C.: The Catholic University of America, 1930.

Benedictus XIV, *De Synodo Dioecesana*, 2. Parmensis ed., 2 vols., Parmae, 1764.

Benko, Matthew, *The Abbot* NULLIUS, The Catholic University of America Canon Law Studies, n. 173, Washington, D. C.: The Catholic University of America Press, 1943.

Bennett, Charles, *New Latin Grammar*, Boston, New York, Chicago, 1918.

Beste, Uldalricus, *Introductio in Codicem*, 2. ed., Collegeville, Minn.: St. John's Abbey Press, 1944.

Blat, Albertus, *Commentarium Textus Codicis Iuris Canonici*, 5 vols. in 6, Vol. II, *De Personis*, Romae, 1919; Vol. VI, *De Delictis et Poenis*, Romae, 1924.

Bouix, Marie Dominique, *De Concilio Provinciali*, 3. ed., Parisiis, 1884.

Bouscaren, T.-Ellis, A., *Canon Law, A Text and Commentary*, Milwaukee: Bruce, 1946.

Brown, Brendan, *The Canonical Juristic Personality with Special Reference to Its Status in the United States of America*, The Catholic University of America Canon Law Studies, n. 39, Washington, D. C.: The Catholic University of America, 1927.

Cavigioli, Joannes, *De Censuris Latae Sententiae Quae in Codice Juris Canonici Continentur Commentariolum*, Torino, 1919.

Ceillier, Remy, *Histoire Générale des Auteurs Sacrés et Eccélsiastiques*, 14 vols. in 17, Paris, 1858-1869.

Chelodi, Ioannes, *Ius de Personis iuxta Codicem Iuris Canonici*, 2. ed., ab E. Bertagnolli recognita et aucta, Tridenti: Libr. Edit. Tridentum, 1927.

———, *Ius Poenale et Ordo Procedendi in Iudiciis Criminalibus iuxta Codicem Iuris Canonici*, Tridenti: Libr. Edit. Tridentum, 1925.

Claeys Boúúaert, F.-Simenon, G., *Manuale Juris Canonici*, 3 vols., Vol. I, 4. ed., Gandae et Leodii: Apud Seminarium, 1934.

Cocchi, Guidus, *Commentarium in Codicem Iuris Canonici*, 8 vols. in 5, Vol. III, 3. ed. recognita, Taurinorum Augustae: Marietti, 1931.

Coleman, John, *The Minister of Confirmation*, The Catholic University of America Canon Law Studies, n. 125, Washington, D. C.: The Catholic University of America Press, 1941.

Coronata, Matthaeus, Conte a, *Compendium Iuris Canonici,* 2 vols., Taurini: Marietti, 1937-1938.

Coronata, Matthaeus, Conte a, *Institutiones Iuris Canonici,* 5 vols., Taurini: Marietti, 1928-1936.

Corpus Scriptorum Ecclesiasticorum Latinorum, 68 vols., incomplete, Vindobonae, 1866—.

Craisson, D., *Manuale Juris Canonici,* 4 vols., 6. ed., Pictavii, 1880.

D'Annibale, Iosephus, *Summula Theologiae Moralis,* 3 vols., 5. ed., diligenter revisa et novissimis SS. Congregationum decretis locupletata, Romae, 1908.

De Angelis, Philippus, *Praelectiones Iuris Canonici,* 2. ed., 5 vols., Romae, 1908.

De Hericourt, Louis, *Les Loix Ecclésiastiques de France,* nouvelle ed., Paris, 1771.

De Meester, A., *Juris Canonici et Juris Canonico-Civilis Compendium,* ed. nova, 3 vols. in 4, Brugis: Sumptibus et Typis Societatis Sancti Augustini, 1921-1928.

Dictionnaire de Droit Canonique (commencé sous la direction de A. Villien et E. Magnin, professeurs à l'Institut Catholique de Paris [1924]; continué sous la direction de A. Amanieu, maître de conférences à l'Université Catholique de Lille [1926], publié sous la direction de R. Naz, professeur de droit aux Facultés Catholiques de Lille [1934]), Paris, 1924—.

Donnelly, Francis, *The Diocesan Synod,* The Catholic University of America Canon Law Studies, n. 74, Washington, D. C.: The Catholic University of America, 1932.

Fagnanus, Prosper, *Commentaria in Quinque Decretalium Libros,* 5 vols. in 4, Venetiis, 1709.

Ferraris, L., *Prompta Bibliotheca, Canonica, Iuridica, Moralis, Theologica, necnon Ascetica, Polemica, Rubricistica, Historica,* ed. Migne, 8 vols., Parisiis, 1860-1863.

Ferreres, Joannes, *Institutiones Canonicae,* 2 vols., 2. ed. correctior et tutior, Barcinone, 1920.

Godfrey, John, *The Right of Patronage According to the Code of Canon Law,* The Catholic University of America Canon Law Studies, n. 21, Washington, D. C.: The Catholic University of America, 1924.

Gousset, Thomas, *Exposition des Principes du Droit Canonique,* Paris, 1859.

Griechischen Christlichen Schriftsteller der ersten drei Jahrhunderte, Die—Eusebius, 7 vols. in 10, Vol. II, pars I (1903), pars II (1908), Leipzig, 1903-1908.

Guilday, Peter, *A History of the Councils of Baltimore,* New York: Macmillan, 1932.

———, *The Life and Times of John England,* 2 vols., New York: The America Press, 1927.

Guilfoyle, Merlin, *Custom,* The Catholic University of America Canon Law Studies, n. 105, Washington, D. C.: The Catholic University of America, 1937.

Guiniven, John, *The Precept of Hearing Mass,* The Catholic University of America Canon Law Studies, n. 158, Washington, D. C.: The Catholic University of America Press, 1942.

Heck, Theodore, *The Curriculum of the Major Seminary in Relation to Contemporary Conditions,* Washington, D. C.: National Catholic Welfare Conference, 1935.

Hefele, C.-Leclercq, H., *Histoire des Conciles* . . . nouvelle traduction française. . . 10 vols. in 19, Paris, 1907-1938.

Hickey, John, *Irregularities and Simple Impediments,* The Catholic University of America Canon Law Studies, n. 7, Washington, D. C.: The Catholic University of America, 1920.

Hinschius, Paul, *Das Kirchenrecht der Katholiken und Protestanten in Deutschland,* 6 vols., Berlin, 1869-1897.

Hostiensis (Henricus de Segusio), *Commentaria in Quinque Decretalium Libros,* 5 vols. in 3, Venetiis, 1581.

Ioannes, Andreae, *In Quinque Decretalium Libros Novella Commentaria,* 5 vols. in 4, Venetiis, 1581.

Jaeger, Leo, *The Administration of Vacant and Quasi-Vacant Episcopal Sees in the United States,* The Catholic University of America Canon Law Studies, n. 81, Washington, D. C.: The Catholic University of America, 1932.

Keene, Michael, *Religious Ordinaries and Canon 198,* The Catholic University of America Canon Law Studies, n. 135, Washington, D. C.: The Catholic University of America Press, 1942.

Kremer, Michael, *Church Support in the United States,* The Catholic University of America Canon Law Studies, n. 61, Washington, D. C.: The Catholic University of America, 1930.

Lega, Michael, *Commentarius in Iudicia Ecclesiastica iuxta Codicem Iuris Canonici,* curante Victorio Bartoccetti, 3 vols., 1938-1941, Vol. I, Romae: Anonima Libraria Cattolica Italiana, 1938.

Lynch, George, *Coadjutors and Auxiliaries of Bishops,* The Catholic University of America Canon Law Studies, n. 238, Washington, D. C.: The Catholic University of America Press, 1947.

McDonough, Thomas, *Apostolic Administrators,* The Catholic University of America Canon Law Studies, n. 139, Washington, D. C.: The Catholic University of America Press, 1941.

Maroto, Philippus, *Institutiones Iuris Canonici ad Normam Novi Codicis,* 2 vols., Matriti-Romae-Barcinone, 1918-1919.

Maupied, Franciscus, *Juris Canonici Universi Compendium,* accurante J. P. Migne, 2 vols., Parisiis, 1861.

Michiels, Gommarus, *Normae Generalis Juris Canonici,* 2 vols., Lublin: Universitas Catholica, 1929.

———, *Principia Generalia de Personis in Ecclesia,* Lublin: Universitas Catholica, 1932.

Migne, Jacques, *Patrologiae Cursus Completus, Series Latina,* 221 vols., Parisiis, 1844-1864.

Moretti, Aloisius, *Caeremoniale iuxta Ritum Romanum seu de Sacris Functionibus Episcopo Celebrante, Assistente, Absente,* 4 vols., Taurini: Marietti, 1936-1939.

Oesterle, Gerardus, *Praelectiones Iuris Canonici,* Vol. I, Romae: In Collegio S. Anselmi, 1931.

Ojetti, Benedictus, *Commentarium in Codicem Iuris Canonici,* 4 vols. in 3, Romae: Apud Aedes Universitatis Gregorianae, 1927-1931.

———, *Synopsis Rerum Moralium et Iuris Pontificii,* 2 vols. in 1, 2. ed., emendata et aucta, Prati, 1904-1905.

Panormitanus, Abbas (Nicolaus de Tudeschis), *Commentaria in Quinque Decretalium Libros,* 7 vols. in 5, Venetiis, 1588.

Petra, Vincentius, *Commentaria ad Constitutiones Apostolicas,* 5 vols. in 2, Venetiis, 1729.

Prümmer, Dominicus, *Manuale Iuris Canonici,* 3. ed. aucta et secundum recentissimas decisiones Romanas recognita, Friburgi Brisgoviae, 1922.

Reilly, Edward, *The General Norms of Dispensation,* The Catholic University of America Canon Law Studies, n. 119, Washington, D. C.: The Catholic University of America Press, 1939.

Roberti, Franciscus, *De Processibus,* 2 vols., Vol. I, 2. ed., 3. impressio, Romae: Apud Custodiam Librariam Pontificii Instituti Utriusque Iuris, 1941.

Rufinus, *Summa Decretorum,* ed. H. Singer, Paderborn, 1902.

Sägmüller, J., *Lehrbuch des Katholischen Kirchenrechts,* 2 vols., 3. ed., Freiburg im Breisgau, 1914.

Santi, F.-Leitner, M., *Praelectiones Juris Canonici,* 5 vols. in 3, 4. ed., Ratisbonae, 1903-1905.

Schaefer, Timotheus, *De Religiosis ad Normam Codicis Iuris Canonici,* 3. ed. aucta et emendata, Romae: Typis Polyglottis Vaticanis, S. A. L. E. R., 1940.

Scherer, Rudolf Ritter von, *Handbuch des Kirchenrechtes,* 2 vols., Graz-Leipzig, 1886-1898.

Schmalzgrueber, Franciscus, *Jus Ecclesiasticum Universum,* 5 vols. in 12, Romae, 1843-1845.

Schmidt, John, *The Principles of Authentic Interpretation in Canon 17 of the Code of Canon Law,* The Catholic University of America Canon Law Studies, n. 141, Washington, D. C.: The Catholic University of America Press, 1941.

Sebastianelli, Guilelmus, *Praelectiones Juris Canonici,* 3 vols., Vol. I, *De Personis,* 2. ed. emendata et aucta, Romae, 1905.

Sipos, Stephanus, *Enchiridion Iuris Canonici,* 2. ed., Pécs: Ex Typographia "Haladás R. T.," 1931.

Smith, S., *Elements of Ecclesiastical Law,* 3 vols., Vol. I, 7. ed., completely revised according to the decrees of the Third Plenary Council of Baltimore, New York, 1887.

Suarez, Franciscus, *Opera Omnia,* 28 vols., ed. Vivès, Parisiis, 1856-1861, Vols. V, VI, *De Legibus et Legislatore Deo.*

Taunton, Ethelred, *The Law of the Church,* London-St. Louis, 1906.

Thomassinus, Ludovicus, *Vetus et Nova Ecclesiae Disciplina circa Beneficia et Beneficiarios,* 3 partes in 10 vols., ed. postrema cum Parisieni accuratissime collata, Magontiaci, 1787.

Toso, Albertus, *Ad Codicem Juris Canonici Commentaria Minora,* 5 vols. in 2, Vol. I, 2. ed. revisa, Torino-Romae, 1921; Vols. II-V, Romae: Jus Pontificium, 1922-1927.

Van Hove, A., *Commentarium Lovaniense in Codicem Iuris Canonici,* Vol. I, Tom. I (*Prolegomena ad Codicem Iuris Canonici*), 2. ed. auctior et emendatior, Mechliniae et Romae: Dessain, 1945; Vol. I, Tom. II (*De Legibus Ecclesiasticis*), 1930.

Vermeersch, A.-Creusen, I., *Epitome Iuris Canonici,* 3 vols., Vol. I, 6. ed., Mechliniae-Romae: Dessain, 1937; Vol. II, 6. ed., 1940; Vol. III, 5. ed., 1936.

Vromant, G., *De Bonis Ecclesiae Temporalibus,* 2. ed., Louvain: Museum Lessianum, 1934.

Wernz, Franciscus X., *Ius Decretalium,* 2. ed., 6 vols., Romae et Prati, 1905-1913.

Wernz, F. X.-Vidal, P., *Ius Canonicum,* 7 vols. in 8, Romae: Apud Aedes Universitatis Gregorianae, 1925-1938; Vol. II, 3. ed., 1943.

Winslow, Francis, *Vicars and Prefects Apostolic,* The Catholic University of America Canon Law Studies, n. 24, Washington, D. C.: The Catholic University of America, 1924.

Woywod, Stanislaus, *A Practical Commentary on the Code of Canon Law,* 2 vols., New York: Wagner, Vol. I, 6. printing, 1941; Vol. II, 5. ed. revised, 1939.

Zaplotnik, Ioannes, *De Vicariis Foraneis,* The Catholic University of America Canon Law Studies, n. 47, Washington, D. C.: The Catholic University of America, 1927.

Articles

Anonymous, "Annotationes"—*Periodica,* XIV (1925), 180-182.

———, "From Foreign Reviews"—*The Clergy Review,* XIV (1938), 89, 90.

Boudinhon, A., "Circa can. 105, n. 1, an nullus semper sit actus non petito consilio"—*Jus Pontificium,* VIII (1928), 29-35.

Creusen, I., "L'effet juridique des consultations,"—*Nouvelle Revue Théologique,* LV (1928), 100-116.

Hanrahan, P., "The Law on Plenary Councils"—*The Clergy Review,* XIV (1938), 387-402.

Maroto, Philippus, "Disposizioni circa le conferenze episcopali in Italia"—*Apollinaris,* V (1932), 277-280.

Nevin, John, "Power of Plenary Council to Reserve Sins"—*The Australasian Catholic Record,* VIII (1931), 228-231.

Roelker, Edward, "The Interpretation of Invalidating Laws"—*The Jurist,* III (1943), 364-403.

Vermeersch, Arthurus, "De munere et officiis vicarii et praefecti apostolici secundum praesens ius"—*Periodica,* IX (1921), (19)-(34).

Periodicals

Apollinaris, Romae, 1928—.

Australasian Catholic Record, The, Manly, 1924—.

Clergy Review, The, London, 1931—.

Jurist, The, Washington, D. C., 1941—.

Jus Pontificium, Romae, 1921—.

Nouvelle Revue Théologique, Tournai, 1869—.

Periodica de Religiosis et Missionariis, 8 vols., Brugis, 1905-1919; from 1920: *Periodica de Re Canonica et Morali Utilia Praesertim Religiosis et Missonariis,* 7 vols., Brugis, 1920-1927; from 1927: *Periodica de Re Morali, Canonica, Liturgica,* Brugis (1927-1936), et Romae (1937—), Vol. XVI, 1927—.

ABBREVIATIONS

AAS—*Acta Apostolicae Sedis.*
Bull. Rom. Taur.—*Bullarium Romanum, ed. Taurinensis.*
Can.—Canon.
Collect.—*Collectanea S.C. de Propaganda Fide.*
Coll. Lac.—*Collectio Lacensis.*
CSEL—*Corpus Scriptorum Ecclesiasticorum Latinorum.*
D.—*Digesta Imperatoris Iustiniani.*
Decr. Auth. S. R. C.—*Decreta Authentica Sacrorum Rituum Congregationis.*
Fontes—*Codicis Iuris Canonici Fontes cura . . . Gasparri editi.*
GCS—*Die Griechischen Christlichen Schriftsteller der ersten drei Jahrhunderte.*
Mansi—*Sacrorum Conciliorum Nova et Amplissima Collectio.*
MGH—*Monumenta Germaniae Historica.*
MGH, Conc.—*Monumenta Germaniae Historica, Legum Sectio III, Concilia.*
P. C. I.—Pontificia Commissio ad Codicis Canones Authentice Interpretandos.
Periodica—*Periodica de Re Morali, Canonica, Liturgica.*
S. C. C.—Sacra Congregatio Concilii.
S. C. Consist.—Sacra Congregatio Consistorialis.
S. C. de Prop. Fide—Sacra Congregatio de Propaganda Fide.
S. R. C.—Sacrorum Rituum Congregatio.
S. C. S. Off.—Sacra Congregatio Sancti Officii.

ALPHABETICAL INDEX

BIOGRAPHICAL NOTE

Francis Joseph Murphy was born in New York City on April 20, 1912. He attended Our Lady of Mercy School, New York City, and Resurrection School in Rye, New York. His high school and college training was received at Fordham Preparatory School and Fordham University, New York City, from which institution he obtained the degree of Bachelor of Arts in June, 1939. His theological studies were completed at St. John's Seminary, Little Rock, Arkansas, and he was ordained to the holy priesthood on December 21, 1943, for the Diocese of Raleigh, North Carolina. In October, 1944, he entered the School of Canon Law of the Catholic University of America, where he received the degree of the Baccalaureate in Canon Law in May, 1945, and the degree of the Licentiate in Canon Law in June, 1946.

CANON LAW STUDIES *

1. FRERIKS, REV. CELESTINE A., C.PP.S., J.C.D., Religious Congregations in Their External Relations, 121 pp., 1916.
2. GALLIHER, REV. DANIEL M., O.P., J.C.D., Canonical Elections, 117 pp., 1917.
3. BORKOWSKI, REV. AURELIUS L., O.F.M., J.C.D., De Confraternitatibus Ecclesiasticis, 136 pp., 1918.
4. CASTILLO, REV. CAYO, J.C.D., Disertacion Historico-Canonica sobre la Potestad del Cabildo en Sede Vacante o Impedida del Vicario Capitular, 99 pp., 1919 (1918).
5. KUBELBECK, REV. WILLIAM J., S.T.B., J.C.D., The Sacred Penitentiaria and Its Relation to Faculties of Ordinaries and Priests, 129 pp., 1918.
6. PETROVITS, REV. JOSEPH, J.C., S.T.D., J.C.D., The New Church Law on Matrimony, X-461 pp., 1919.
7. HICKEY, REV. JOHN J., S.T.B., J.C.D., Irregularities and Simple Impediments in the New Code of Canon Law, 100 pp., 1920.
8. KLEKOTKA, REV. PETER J., S.T.B., J.C.D., Diocesan Consultors, 179 pp., 1920.
9. WANENMACHER, REV. FRANCIS, J.C.D., The Evidence in Ecclesiastical Procedure Affecting the Marriage Bond, 1920 (Printed 1935).
10. GOLDEN, REV. HENRY FRANCIS, J.C.D., Parochial Benefices in the New Code, IV-119 pp., 1921 (Printed 1925).
11. KOUDELKA, REV. CHARLES J., J.C.D., Pastors, Their Rights and Duties According to the New Code of Canon Law, 211 pp., 1921.
12. MELO, REV. ANTONIUS, O.F.M., J.C.D., De Exemptione Regularium, X-188 pp., 1921.
13. SCHAAF, REV. VALENTINE THEODORE, O.F.M., S.T.B., J.C.D., The Cloister, X-180 pp., 1921.
14. BURKE, REV. THOMAS JOSEPH, S.T.D., J.C.D., Competence in Ecclesiastical Tribunals, IV-117 pp., 1922.
15. LEECH, REV. GEORGE LEO, J.C.D., A Comparative Study of the Constitution "Apostolicae Sedis" and the "Codex Juris Canonici," 179 pp., 1922.
16. MOTRY, REV. HUBERT LOUIS, S.T.D., J.C.D., Diocesan Faculties According to the Code of Canon Law, II-167 pp., 1922.
17. MURPHY, REV. GEORGE LAWRENCE, J.C.D., Delinquencies and Penalties in the Administration and the Reception of the Sacraments, IV-121 pp., 1923.
18. O'REILLY, REV. JOHN ANTHONY, S.T.B., J.C.D., Ecclesiastical Sepulture in the New Code of Canon Law, II-129 pp., 1923.

* From nn. 1-100 inclusive only n. 25 is still obtainable.

From n. 101 onward all numbers are available except the following: nn. 101-114 inclusive, and also nn. 116, 118, 120, 122, 123 and 162.

19. MICHALICKA, REV. WENCESLAS CYRILL, O.S.B., J.C.D., Judicial Procedure in Dismissal of Clerical Exempt Religious, 107 pp., 1923.
20. DARGIN, REV. EDWARD VINCENT, S.T.B., J.C.D., Reserved Cases According to the Code of Canon Law, IV-103 pp., 1924.
21. GODFREY, REV. JOHN A., S.T.B., J.C.D., The Right of Patronage According to the Code of Canon Law, 153 pp., 1924.
22. HAGEDORN, REV. FRANCIS EDWARD, J.C.D., General Legislation on Indulgences, II-154 pp., 1924.
23. KING, REV. JAMES IGNATIUS, J.C.D., The Administration of the Sacraments to Dying Non-Catholics, V-141 pp., 1924.
24. WINSLOW, REV. FRANCIS JOSEPH, O.F.M., J.C.D., Vicars and Prefects Apostolic, IV-149 pp., 1924.
25. CORREA, REV. JOSE SERVELION, S.T.L., J.C.D., La Potestad Legislativa de la Iglesia Catolica, IV-127 pp., 1925.
26. DUGAN, REV. HENRY FRANCIS, A.M., J.C.D., The Judiciary Department of the Diocesan Curia, 87 pp., 1925.
27. KELLER, REV. CHARLES FREDERICK, S.T.B., J.C.D., Mass Stipends, 167 pp., 1925.
28. PASCHANG, REV. JOHN LINUS, J.C.D., The Sacramentals According to the Code of Canon Law, 129 pp., 1925.
29. PIONTEK, REV. CYRILLUS, O.F.M., S.T.B., J.C.D., De Indulto Exclaustrationis necnon Saecularizationis, XIII-289 pp., 1925.
30. KEARNEY, REV. RICHARD JOSEPH, S.T.B., J.C.D., Sponsors at Baptism According to the Code of Canon Law, IV-127 pp., 1925.
31. BARTLETT, REV. CHESTER JOSEPH, A.M., LL.B., J.C.D., The Tenure of Parochial Property in the United States of America, V-108 pp., 1926.
32. KILKER, REV. ADRIAN JEROME, J.C.D., Extreme Unction, V-425 pp., 1926.
33. MCCORMICK, REV. ROBERT EMMETT, J.C.D., Confessors of Religious, VIII-266 pp., 1926.
34. MILLER, REV. NEWTON THOMAS, J.C.D., Founded Masses According to the Code of Canon Law, VII-93 pp., 1926.
35. ROELKER, REV. EDWARD G., S.T.D., J.C.D., Principles of Privilege According to the Code of Canon Law, XI-166 pp., 1926.
36. BAKALARCZYK, REV. RICHARDUS, M.I.C., J.U.D., De Novitiatu, VIII-208 pp., 1927.
37. PIZZUTI, REV. LAWRENCE, O.F.M., J.U.L., De Parochis Religiosis, 1927. (Not Printed.)
38. BLILEY, REV. NICHOLAS MARTIN, O.S.B., J.C.D., Altars According to the Code of Canon Law, XIX-132 pp., 1927.
39. BROWN, MR. BRENDAN FRANCIS, A.B., LL.M., J.U.D., The Canonical Juristic Personality with Special Reference to its Status in the United States of America, V-212 pp., 1927.
40. CAVANAUGH, REV. WILLIAM THOMAS, C.P., J.U.D., The Reservation of the Blessed Sacrament, VIII-101 pp., 1927.

41. BOHENY, REV. WILLIAM J., C.S.C., A.B., J.U.D., Church Property: Modes of Acquisition, X-118 pp., 1927.
42. FELDHAUS, REV. ALOYSIUS H., C.PP.S., J.C.D., Oratories, IX-141 pp., 1927.
43. KELLY, REV. JAMES PATRICK, A.B., J.C.D., The Jurisdiction of the Simple Confessor, X-208 pp., 1927.
44. NEUBERGER, REV. NICHOLAS J., J.C.D., Canon 6 or the Relation of the Codex Juris Canonici to the Preceding Legislation, V-95 pp., 1927.
45. O'KEEFE, REV. GERALD MICHAEL, J.C.D., Matrimonial Dispensations, Powers of Bishops, Priests, and Confessors, VIII-232 pp., 1927.
46. QUIGLEY, REV. JOSEPH A. M., A.B., J.C.D., Condemned Societies, 139 pp., 1927.
47. ZAPLOTNIK, REV. JOHANNES LEO, J.C.D., De Vicariis Foraneis, X-142 pp., 1927.
48. DUSKIE, REV. JOHN ALOYSIUS, A.B., J.C.D., The Canonical Status of the Orientals in the United States, VIII-196 pp., 1928.
49. HYLAND, REV. FRANCIS EDWARD, J.C.D., Excommunication, Its Nature, Historical Development and Effects, VIII-181 pp., 1928.
50. REINMANN, REV. GERALD JOSEPH, O.M.C., J.C.D., The Third Order Secular of Saint Francis, 201 pp., 1928.
51. SCHENK, REV. FRANCIS J., J.C.D., The Matrimonial Impediments of Mixed Religion and Disparity of Cult, XVI-318 pp., 1929.
52. COADY, REV. JOHN JOSEPH, S.T.D., J.U.D., A.M., The Appointment of Pastors, VIII-150 pp., 1929.
53. KAY, REV. THOMAS HENRY, J.C.D., Competence in Matrimonial Procedure, VIII-164 pp., 1929.
54. TURNER, REV. SIDNEY JOSEPH, C.P., J.U.D., The Vow of Poverty, XLIX-217 pp., 1929.
55. KEARNEY, REV. RAYMOND A., A.B., S.T.D., J.C.D., The Principles of Delegation, VII-149 pp., 1929.
56. CONRAN, REV. EDWARD JAMES, A.B., J.C.D., The Interdict, V-163 pp., 1930.
57. O'NEILL, REV. WILLIAM H., J.C.D., Papal Rescripts of Favor, VII-218 pp., 1930.
58. BASTNAGEL, REV. CLEMENT VINCENT, J.U.D., The Appointment of Parochial Adjutants and Assistants, XV-257 pp., 1930.
59. FERRY, REV. WILLIAM A., A.B., J.C.D., Stole Fees, V-136 pp., 1930.
60. COSTELLO, REV. JOHN MICHAEL, A.B., J.C.D., Domicile and Quasi-Domicile, VII-201 pp., 1930.
61. KREMER, REV. MICHAEL NICHOLAS, A.B., S.T.B., J.C.D., Church Support in the United States, VI-136 pp., 1930.
62. ANGULO, REV. LUIS, C.M., J.C.D., Legislation de la Iglesia sobre la intencion en la application de la Santa Misa, VII-104 pp., 1931.
63. FREY, REV. WOLFGANG NORBERT, O.S.B., A.B., J.C.D., The Act of Religious Profession, VIII-174 pp., 1931.

64. Roberts, Rev. James Brendan, A.B., J.C.D., The Banns of Marriage, XIV-140 pp., 1931.
65. Ryder, Rev. Raymond Aloysius, A.B., J.C.D., Simony, IX-151 pp., 1931.
66. Campagna, Rev. Angelo, Ph.D., J.U.D., Il Vicario Generale del Vescovo, VII-205 pp., 1931.
67. Cox, Rev. Joseph Godfrey, A.B., J.C.D., The Administration of Seminaries, VI-124 pp., 1931.
68. Gregory, Rev. Donald J., J.U.D., The Pauline Privilege, XV-165 pp., 1931.
69. Donohue, Rev. John F., J.C.D., The Impediment of Crime, VII-110 pp., 1931.
70. Dooley, Rev. Eugene A., O.M.I., J.C.D., Church Law on Sacred Relics, IX-143 pp., 1931.
71. Orth, Rev. Clement Raymond, O.M.C., J.C.D., The Approbation of Religious Institutes, 171 pp., 1931.
72. Pernicone, Rev. Joseph M., A.B., J.C.D., The Ecclesiastical Prohibition of Books, XII-267 pp., 1932.
73. Clinton, Rev. Connell, A.B., J.C.D., The Paschal Precept, IX-108 pp., 1932.
74. Donnelly, Rev. Francis B., A.M., S.T.L., J.C.D., The Diocesan Synod, VIII-125 pp., 1932.
75. Torrente, Rev. Camilo, C.M.F., J.C.D., Las Procesiones Sagradas, V-145 pp., 1932.
76. Murphy, Rev. Edwin J., C.PP.S., J.C.D., Suspension Ex Informata Conscientia, XI-122 pp., 1932.
77. MacKenzie, Rev. Eric F., A.M., S.T.L., J.C.D., The Delict of Heresy in its Commission, Penalization, Absolution, VII-124 pp., 1932.
78. Lyons, Rev. Avitus E., S.T.B., J.C.D., The Collegiate Tribunal of First Instance, XI-147 pp., 1932.
79. Connolly, Rev. Thomas A., J.C.D., Appeals, XI-195, pp., 1932.
80. Sangmeister, Rev. Joseph V., A.B., J.C.D., Force and Fear as Precluding Matrimonial Consent, V-211 pp., 1932.
81. Jaeger, Rev. Leo A., A.B., J.C.D., The Administration of Vacant and Quasi-Vacant Episcopal Sees in the United States, IX-229 pp., 1932.
82. Rimlinger, Rev. Herbert T., J.C.D., Error Invalidating Matrimonial Consent, VII-79 pp., 1932.
83. Barrett, Rev. John D. M., S.S., J.C.D., A Comparative Study of the Councils of Baltimore and the Code of Canon Law, X-223 pp., 1932.
84. Carberry, Rev. John J., Ph.D., S.T.D., J.C.D., The Juridical Form of Marriage, X-177 pp., 1934.
85. Dolan, Rev. John L., A.B., J.C.D., The Defensor Vinculi, XII-157 pp., 1934.
86. Hannan, Rev. Jerome D., A.M., S.T.D., LL.B., J.C.D., The Canon Law of Wills, IX-517 pp., 1934.

87. Lemieux, Rev. Delise A., A.M., J.C.D., The Sentence in Ecclesiastical Procedure, IX-131 pp., 1934.
88. O'Rourke, Rev. James J., A.B., J.C.D., Parish Registers, VII-109 pp., 1934.
89. Timlin, Rev. Bartholomew, O.F.M., A.M., J.C.D., Conditional Matrimonial Consent, X-381 pp., 1934.
90. Wahl, Rev. Francis X., A.B., J.C.D., The Matrimonial Impediments of Consanguinity and Affinity, VI-125 pp., 1934.
91. White, Rev. Robert J., A.B., LL.B., S.T.B., J.C.D., Canonical Ante-Nuptial Promises and the Civil Law, VI-152 pp., 1934.
92. Herrera, Rev. Antonio Parra, O.C.D., J.C.D., Legislacion Ecclesiastica sobra el Ayuno y la Abstinencia, XI-191 pp., 1935.
93. Kennedy, Rev. Edwin J., J.C.D., The Special Matrimonial Process in Cases of Evident Nullity, X-165 pp., 1935.
94. Manning, Rev. John J., A.B., J.C.D., Presumption of Law in Matrimonial Procedure, XI-111 pp., 1935.
95. Moeder, Rev. John M., J.C.D., The Proper Bishop for Ordination and Dismissorial Letters, VII-135 pp., 1935.
96. O'Mara, Rev. William A., A.B., J.C.D., Canonical Causes for Matrimonial Dispensations, IX-155 pp., 1935.
97. Reilly, Rev. Peter, J.C.D., Residence of Pastors, IX-81 pp., 1935.
98. Smith, Rev. Mariner T., O.P., S.T.Lr., J.C.D., The Penal Law for Religious, VIII-169 pp., 1935.
99. Whalen, Rev. Donald W., A.M., J.C.D., The Value of Testimonial Evidence in Matrimonial Procedure, XIII-297 pp., 1935.
100. Cleary, Rev. Jóseph F., J.C.D., Canonical Limitations on the Alienation of Church Property, VIII-141 pp., 1936.
101. Glynn, Rev. John C., J.C.D., The Promoter of Justice, XX-337 pp., 1936.
102. Brennan, Rev. James H., S.S., M.A., S.T.B., J.C.D., The Simple Convalidation of Marriage, VI-135 pp., 1937.
103. Brunini, Rev. Joseph Bernard, J.C.D., The Clerical Obligations of Canons 139 and 142, X-121 pp., 1937.
104. Connor, Rev. Maurice, A.B., J.C.D., The Administrative Removal of Pastors, VIII-159 pp., 1937.
105. Guilfoyle, Rev. Merlin Joseph, J.C.D., Custom, XI-144 pp., 1937.
106. Hughes, Rev. James Austin, A.B., A.M., J.C.D., Witnesses in Criminal Trials of Clerics, IX-140 pp., 1937.
107. Jansen, Rev. Raymond J., A.B., S.T.L., J.C.D., Canonical Provisions for Catechetical Instruction, VII-153 pp., 1937.
108. Kealy, Rev. John James, A.B., J.C.D., The Introductory Libellus in Church Court Procedure, XI-121 pp., 1937.
109. McManus, Rev. James Edward, C.SS.R., J.C.D., The Administration of Temporal Goods in Religious Institutes, XVI-196 pp., 1937.

110. MORIARTY, REV. EUGENE JAMES, J.C.D., Oaths in Ecclesiastical Courts, X-115 pp., 1937.
111. RAINER, REV. ELIGIUS GEORGE, C.SS.R., J.C.D., Suspension of Clerics, XVII-249 pp., 1937.
112. REILLY, REV. THOMAS F., C.SS.R., J.C.D., Visitation of Religious, VI-195 pp., 1938.
113. MORIARTY, REV. FRANCIS E., C.SS.R., J.C.D., The Extraordinary Absolution from Censures, XV-334 pp., 1938.
114. CONNOLLY, REV. NICHOLAS P., J.C.D., The Canonical Erection of Parishes, X-132 pp., 1938.
115. DONOVAN, REV. JAMES JOSEPH, J.C.D., The Pastor's Obligation in Prenuptial Investigation, XII-322 pp., 1938.
116. HARRIGAN, REV. ROBERT J., M.A., S.T.B., J.C.D., The Radical Sanation of Invalid Marriages, VIII-208 pp., 1938.
117. BOFFA, REV. CONRAD HUMBERT, J.C.D., Canonical Provisions for Catholic Schools, VII-211 pp., 1939.
118. PARSONS, REV. ANSCAR JOHN, O.M.Cap., J.C.D., Canonical Elections, XII-236 pp., 1939.
119. REILLY, REV. EDWARD MICHAEL, A.B., J.C.D., The General Norms of Dispensation, XII-156 pp., 1939.
120. RYAN, REV. GERALD ALOYSIUS, A.B., J.C.D., Principles of Episcopal Jurisdiction, XII-172 pp., 1939.
121. BURTON, REV. FRANCIS JAMES, C.S.C., A.B., J.C.D., A Commentary on Canon 1125, X-222 pp., 1940.
122. MIASKIEWICZ, REV. FRANCIS SIGISMUND, J.C.D., Supplied Jurisdiction According to Canon 209, XII-340 pp., 1940.
123. RICE, REV. PATRICK WILLIAM, A.B., J.C.D., Proof of Death in Prenuptial Investigation, VIII-156 pp., 1940.
124. ANGLIN, REV. THOMAS FRANCIS, M.S., J.C.D., The Eucharistic Fast, VIII-183 pp., 1941.
125. COLEMAN, REV. JOHN JEROME, J.C.D., The Minister of Confirmation, VI-153 pp., 1941.
126. DOWNS, REV. JOHN EMMANUEL, A.B., J.C.D., The Concept of Clerical Immunity, XI-163 pp., 1941.
127. ESSWEIN, REV. ANTHONY ALBERT, J.C.D., Extrajudicial Penal Powers of Ecclesiastical Superiors, X-144 pp., 1941.
128. FARRELL, REV. BENJAMIN FRANCIS, M.A., S.T.L., J.C.D., The Rights and Duties of the Local Ordinary Regarding Congregations of Women Religious of Pontifical Approval, V-195 pp., 1941.
129. FEENEY, REV. THOMAS JOHN, A.B., S.T.L., J.C.D., Restitutio in Integrum, VI-169 pp., 1941.
130. FINDLAY, REV. STEPHEN WILLIAM, O.S.B., A.B., J.C.D., Canonical Norms Governing the Deposition and Degradation of Clerics, XVII-279 pp., 1941.

131. GOODWINE, REV. JOHN, A.B., S.T.L., J.C.D., The Right of the Church to Acquire Property, VIII-119 pp., 1941.
132. HESTON, REV. EDWARD LOUIS, C.S.C., Ph.D., S.T.D., J.C.D., The Alienation of Church Property in the United States, XII-222 pp., 1941.
133. HOGAN, REV. JAMES JOHN, A.B., S.T.L., J.C.D., Judicial Advocates and Procurators, XIII-200 pp., 1941.
134. KEALY, REV. THOMAS M., A.B., Litt.B., J.C.D., Dowry of Women Religious, IX-152 pp., 1941.
135. KEENE, REV. MICHAEL JAMES, O.S.B., J.C.D., Religious Ordinaries and Canon 198, V-164 pp., 1942.
136. KERIN, REV. CHARLES A., S.S., M.A., S.T.B., J.C.D., The Privation of Christian Burial, XVI-279 pp., 1941.
137. LOUIS, REV. WILLIAM FRANCIS, M.A., J.C.D., Diocesan Archives, X-101 pp., 1941.
138. McDEVITT, REV. GILBERT JOSEPH, A.B., J.C.D., Legitimacy and Legitimation, X-247 pp., 1941.
139. McDONOUGH, REV. THOMAS JOSEPH, A.B., J.C.D., Apostolic Administrators, X-217 pp., 1941.
140. MEIER, REV. CARL ANTHONY, A.B., J.C.D., Penal Administrative Procedure Against Negligent Pastors, XI-240 pp., 1941.
141. SCHMIDT, REV. JOHN ROGG, A.B., J.C.D., The Principles of Authentic Interpretation in Canon 17 of the Code of Canon Law, XII-331 pp., 1941.
142. SLAFKOSKY, REV. ANDREW LEONARD, A.B., J.C.D., The Canonical Episcopal Visitation of the Diocese, X-197 pp., 1941.
143. SWOBODA, REV. INNOCENT ROBERT, O.F.M., J.C.D., Ignorance in Relation to the Imputability of Delicts, IX-271 pp., 1941.
144. DUBÉ, REV. ARTHUR JOSEPH, A.B., J.C.D., The General Principles for the Reckoning of Time in Canon Law, VIII-299 pp., 1941.
145. McBRIDE, REV. JAMES T., A.B., J.C.D., Incardination and Excardination of Seculars, XX-585 pp., 1941.
146. KRÓL, REV. JOHN T., J.C.D., The Defendant in Ecclesiastical Trials, XII-207 pp., 1942.
147. COMYNS, REV. JOSEPH J., C.SS.R., A.B., J.C.D., Papal and Episcopal Administration of Church Property, XIV-155 pp., 1942.
148. BARRY, REV. GARRETT FRANCIS, O.M.I., J.C.D., Violation of the Cloister, XII-260 pp., 1942.
149. BOLDUC, REV. GATIEN, C.S.V., A.B., S.T.L., J.C.D., Les Études dans les Religions Cléricales, VIII-155 pp., 1942.
150. BOYLE, REV. DAVID JOHN, M.A., J.C.D., The Juridic Effects of Moral Certitude on Pre-Nuptial Guarantees, XII-188 pp., 1942.
151. CANAVAN, REV. WALTER JOSEPH, M.A., Litt.D., J.C.D., The Profession of Faith, XII-143 pp., 1942.
152. DESROCHERS, REV. BRUNO, A.B., Ph.L., S.T.B., J.C.D., Le Premier Concile Plénier de Québec et le Code de Droit Canonique, XIV-186 pp., 1942.

153. Dillon, Rev. Robert Edward, A.B., J.C.D., Common Law Marriage, X-148 pp., 1942.
154. Dodwell, Rev. Edward John, Ph.D., S.T.B., J.C.D., The Time and Place for the Celebration of Marriage, X-156 pp., 1942.
155. Donnellan, Rev. Thomas Andrew, A.B., J.C.D., The Obligation of the Missa pro Populo, VII-131 pp., 1942.
156. Eltz, Rev. Louis Anthony, A.B., J.C.D., Cooperation in Crime, XII-208 pp., 1942.
157. Gass, Rev. Sylvester Francis, M.A., J.C.D., Ecclesiastical Pensions, XI-206 pp., 1942.
158. Guiniven, Rev. John Joseph, C.SS.R., J.C.D., The Precept of Hearing Mass, XIV-188 pp., 1942.
159. Gulczynski, Rev. John Theophilus, J.C.D., The Desecration and Violation of Churches, X-126 pp., 1942.
160. Hammill, Rev. John Leo, M.A., J.C.D., The Obligations of the Traveler According to Canon 14, VIII-204 pp., 1942.
161. Haydt, Rev. John Joseph, A.B., J.C.D., Reserved Benefices, XI-148 pp., 1942.
162. Huser, Rev. Roger John, O.F.M., A.B., J.C.D., The Crime of Abortion in Canon Law, XII-187 pp., 1942.
163. Kearney, Rev. Francis Patrick, A.B., S.T.L., J.C.D., The Principles of Canon 1127, X-162 pp., 1942.
164. Linahen, Rev. Leo James, S.T.L., J.C.D., De Absolutione Complicis in Peccato Turpi, V-114 pp., 1942.
165. McCloskey, Rev. Joseph Aloysius, A.B., J.C.D., The Subject of Ecclesiastical Law According to Canon 12, XVII-246 pp., 1942.
166. O'Neill, Rev. Francis Joseph, C.SS.R., J.C.D., The Dismissal of Religious in Temporary Vows, XIII-220 pp., 1942.
167. Prince, Rev. John Edward, A.B., S.T.B., J.C.D., The Diocesan Chancellor, X-136 pp., 1942.
168. Riesner, Rev. Albert Joseph, C.SS.R., J.C.D., Apostates and Fugitives from Religious Institutes, IX-168 pp., 1942.
169. Stenger, Rev. Joseph Bernard, J.C.D., The Mortgaging of Church Property, 186 pp., 1942.
170. Waldron, Rev. Joseph Francis, A.B., J.C.D., The Minister of Baptism, XII-197 pp., 1942.
171. Willett, Rev. Robert Albert, J.C.D., The Probative Value of Documents in Ecclesiastical Trials, X-124 pp., 1942.
172. Woeber, Rev. Edward Martin, M.A., J.C.D., The Interpellations, XII-161 pp., 1942.
173. Benko, Rev. Matthew Aloysius, O.S.B., M.A., J.C.D., The Abbot *Nullius*, XVI-148 pp., 1943.
174. Christ, Rev. Joseph James, M.A., S.T.L., J.C.D., Dispensation from Vindicative Penalties, XIV-285 pp., 1943.

175. CLANCY, REV. PATRICK M. J., O.P., A.B., S.T.Lr., J.C.D., The Local Religious Superior, X-229 pp., 1943.
176. CLARKE, REV. THOMAS JAMES, J.C.D., Parish Societies, XII-147 pp., 1943.
177. CONNOLLY, REV. JOHN PATRICK, S.T.L., J.C.D., Synodal Examiners and Parish Priest Consultors, X-223 pp., 1943.
178. DRUMM, REV. WILLIAM MARTIN, A.B., J.C.D., Hospital Chaplains, XII-175 pp., 1943.
179. FLANAGAN, REV. BERNARD JOSEPH, A.B., S.T.L., J.C.D., The Canonical Erection of Religious Houses, X-147 pp., 1943.
180. KELLEHER, REV. STEPHEN JOSEPH, A.B., S.T.B., J.C.D., Discussions with Non-Catholics: Canonical Legislation, X-93 pp., 1943.
181. LEWIS, REV. GORDIAN, C.P., J.C.D., Chapters in Religious Institutes, XII-169 pp., 1943.
182. MARX, REV. ADOLPH, J.C.D., The Declaration of Nullity of Marriages Contracted Outside the Church, X-151 pp., 1943.
183. MATULENAS, REV. RAYMOND ANTHONY, O.S.B., A.B., J.C.D., Communication, a Source of Privileges, XII-225 pp., 1943.
184. O'LEARY, REV. CHARLES GERARD, C.SS.R., J.C.D., Religious Dismissed After Perpetual Profession, X-213 pp., 1943.
185. POWER, REV. CORNELIUS MICHAEL, J.C.D., The Blessing of Cemeteries, XII-231 pp., 1943.
186. SHUHLER, REV. RALPH VINCENT, O.S.A., J.C.D., Privileges of Religious to Absolve and Dispense, XII-195 pp., 1943.
187. ZIOLKOWSKI, REV. THADDEUS STANISLAUS, A.B., J.C.D., The Consecration and Blessing of Churches, XII-151 pp., 1943.
188. HENEGHAN, REV. JOHN JOSEPH, S.T.D., J.C.D., The Marriages of Unworthy Catholics: Canons 1065 and 1066, XVI-213 pp., 1944.
189. CARROLL, REV. COLEMAN FRANCIS, M.A., S.T.L., J.C.L., Charitable Institutions.
190. CIESLUK, REV. JOSEPH EDWARD, PH.B., S.T.L., J.C.L., National Parishes in the United States.
191. COBURN, REV. VINCENT PAUL, A.B., J.C.D., Marriages of Conscience, XII-172 pp., 1944.
192. CONNORS, REV. CHARLES PAUL, C.S.SP., A.B., J.C.D., Extra-Judicial Procurators in the Code of Canon Law, X-94 pp., 1944.
193. COYLE, REV. PAUL RAYMOND, A.B., J.C.D., Judicial Exceptions, X-142 pp., 1944.
194. FAIR, REV. BARTHOLOMEW FRANCIS, A.B., S.T.L., J.C.D., The Impediment of Abduction, XII-122 pp., 1944.
195. GALLAGHER, REV. THOMAS RAPHAEL, O.P., A.B., S.T.LR., J.C.D., The Examination of the Qualities of the Ordinand, X-166 pp., 1944.
196. GANNON, REV. JOHN MARK, S.T.L., J.C.D., The Interstices Required for the Promotion to Orders, XII-100 pp., 1944.

197. Goldsmith, Rev. J. William, B.C.S., S.T.L., J.C.D., The Competence of Church and State Over Marriages—Disputed Points, X-128 pp., 1944.

198. Goodwine, Rev. Joseph Gerard, A.B., S.T.B., J.C.D., The Reception of Converts, XIV-326 pp., 1944.

199. Kowalski, Rev. Romuald Eugene, O.F.M., A.B., J.C.D., Sustenance of Religious Houses of Regulars, X-174 pp., 1944.

200. McCoy, Rev. Alan Edward, O.F.M., J.C.D., Force and Fear in Relation to Delictual Imputability and Penal Responsibility, XII-160 pp., 1944.

201. McDevitt, Rev. Vincent John, Ph.B., S.T.L., J.C.L., Perjury.

202. Martin, Rev. Thomas Owen, Ph.D., S.T.D., J.C.D., Adverse Possession, Prescription and Limitation of Actions: The Canonical "Praescriptio," XX-208 pp., 1944.

203. Miklosovic, Rev. Paul John, A.B., J.C.L., Attempted Marriages and Their Consequent Juridic Effects.

204. Mundy, Rev. Thomas Maurice, A.B., S.T.L., J.C.D., The Union of Parishes, X-164 pp., 1944.

205. O'Dea, Rev. John Coyle, A.B., J.C.D., The Matrimonial Impediment of Nonage, VIII-126 pp., 1944.

206. Olalia, Rev. Alexander Ayson, S.T.L., J.C.D., A Comparative Study of the Christian Constitution of States and the Constitution of the Philippine Commonwealth, XII-136 pp., 1944.

207. Poisson, Rev. Pierre-Marie, C.S.C., A.B., Ph.L., Th.L., J.C.L., Droits Patrimoniaux des Maisons et des Eglises Religieuses.

208. Stadalnikas, Rev. Casimir Joseph, M.I.C., J.C.D., Reservation of Censures, X-141 pp., 1944.

209. Sullivan, Rev. Eugene Henry, S.T.L., J.C.D., Proof of the Reception of the Sacraments, X-165 pp., 1944.

210. Vaughan, Rev. William Edward, J.C.D., Constitutions for Diocesan Courts, X-210 pp., 1944.

211. Paro, Rev. Gino, S.T.D., J.C.L., The Right of Apostolic Legation.

212. Balzer, Rev. Ralph Francis, C.P., J.C.D., The Computation of Time in a Canonical Novitiate, X-227 pp., 1945.

213. Dougherty, Rev. John Whelan, A.B., S.T.L., J.C.D., De Inquisitione Speciali, XII-195 pp., 1945.

214. Dziob, Rev. Michael Walter, J.C.D., The Sacred Congregation for the Oriental Church, XII-181 pp., 1945.

215. Eidenschink, Rev. John Albert, O.S.B., B.A., J.C.D., The Election of Bishops in the Letters of Pope Gregory the Great, VIII-200 pp., 1945.

216. Gill, Rev. Nicholas, C.P., J.C.D., The Spiritual Prefect in Clerical Religious Houses of Study, X-140 pp., 1945.

217. Hynes, Rev. Harry Gerard, S.T.L., J.C.D., The Privileges of Cardinals, XII-183 pp., 1945.

218. McDevitt, Rev. Gerald Vincent, S.T.L., J.C.D., The Renunciation of an Ecclesiastical Office, XIV-179 pp., 1945.

219. MANNING, REV. JOSEPH LEROY, J.C.D., The Free Conferral of Offices, VII-116 pp., 1945.
220. MEYER, REV. LOUIS G., O.S.B., A.B., S.T.B., J.C.D., Alms-gathering by Religious, XII-163 pp., 1945.
221. O'DONNELL, REV. CLETUS FRANCIS, M.A., J.C.D., The Marriage of Minors, XII-268 pp., 1945.
222. PRUNSKIS, REV. JOSEPH, J.C.D., Comparative Law, Ecclesiastical and Civil, in Lithuanian Concordat, X-161 pp., 1945.
223. SWEENEY, REV. FRANCIS PATRICK, C.SS.R., J.C.D., The Reduction of Clerics to the Lay State, X-199 pp., 1945.
224. VOGELPOHL, REV. HENRY JOHN, J.C.D., The Simple Impediments to Holy Orders, XVI-190 pp., 1945.
225. BROCKHAUS, REV. THOMAS AQUINAS, O.S.B., J.C.D., Religious who are known as *Conversi,* X-127 pp., 1945.
226. GRIESE, REV. ORVILLE NICHOLAS, S.T.D., J.C.D., Marriage and the Procreation of Offspring, XVI-224 pp., 1945.
227. BOUDREAUX, REV. WARREN LOUIS, J.C.L., The *"ab acatholicis nati"* of Canon 1099, § 2.
228. BOWE, REV. THOMAS JOSEPH, A.B., J.C.L., Religious Superioresses.
229. DIEDERICHS, REV. MICHAEL FERDINAND, S.C.J., J.C.D., The Jurisdiction of the Latin Ordinaries over their Oriental Subjects, XIV-153 pp., 1946.
230. DINGMAN, REV. MAURICE JOHN, A.B., S.T.L., J.C.L., The Plaintiff in Contentious Trials.
231. FRISON, REV. BASIL, C.M.F., M.Mus., J.C.D., The Retroactivity of Law, X-221 pp., 1946.
232. GALVIN, REV. WILLIAM ANTHONY, M.A., J.C.D., The Administrative Transfer of Pastors, XII-288 pp., 1946.
233. GORACY, REV. JOSEPH C., J.C.L., The Diriment Matrimonial Impediment of Major Orders.
234. HALE, REV. JOSEPH FRANCIS, M.A., S.T.L., J.C.L., The Pastor of Burial.
235. HENRY, REV. JOSEPH ARTHUR, A.B., J.C.D., The Mass and Holy Communion: Interritual Law, XII-138 pp., 1946.
236. LINENBERGER, REV. HERBERT, C.PP.S., J.C.L., The False Denunciation of an Innocent Confessor.
237. LOWRY, REV. JAMES MARTIN, A.B., J.C.D., Dispensation from Private Vows, XII-216 pp., 1946.
238. LYNCH, REV. GEORGE EDWARD, A.B., S.T.L., J.C.D., Coadjutors and Auxiliaries of Bishops, X-107 pp., 1947.
239. LYNCH, REV. TIMOTHY, M.S.SS.T., J.C.D., Contracts between Bishops and Religious Congregations, XIII-232 pp., 1946.
240. McCLUNN, REV. JUSTIN DAVID, A.B., S.T.L., J.C.D., Administrative Recourse, VII-142 pp., 1946.

241. LOHMULLER, REV. MARTIN NICHOLAS, A.B., J.C.D., The Promulgation of Law, XII-140 pp., 1947.

242. MCGRATH, REV. JAMES, A.B., J.C.D., The Privilege of the Canon, XII-156 pp., 1946.

243. MARBACH, REV. JOSEPH FRANCIS, A.B., J.C.D., Marriage Legislation for the Catholics of the Oriental Rites in the United States and Canada, XIV-314 pp., 1946.

244. SHIMKUS, REV. BERNARD ALOYSIUS, A.B., J.C.L., The Determination and Transfer of Rite.

245. SMITH, REV. VINCENT MICHAEL, A.B., S.T.L., J.C.L., Ignorance Affecting Matrimonial Consent.

246. WACHTRLE, REV. PAUL ANTHONY, A.B., J.C.L., The Baptism of the Children of Non-Catholics.

247. CROTTY, REV. MATTHEW M., J.C.L., The Recipient of First Holy Communion.

248. EAGLETON, REV. GEORGE, J.C.L., The Quinquennial Faculties, Formula IV.

249. GIBBONS, REV. MARION L., C.M., LL.B., J.C.L., Domicile of the Wife Unlawfully Separated from Her Husband.

250. KELLY. REV. BERNARD M., S.T.L., J.C.L., The Functions Reserved to Pastors.

251. KILCULLEN, REV. THOMAS J., LL.M., J.C.L., The Collegiate Moral Person as Party Litigant.

252. LAFONTAINE, REV. GERMAIN J., W.F., J.C.L., Relations Canoniques entre Le Missionnaire et Ses Superieurs.

253. LANE, REV. LORAS T., A.B., S.T.L., J.C.L., Matrimonial Procedure in the Ordinary Court of Second Instance.

254. LOVER, REV. JAMES F., C.SS.R., J.C.L., The Master of Novices.

255. MCNICHOLAS, REV. TIMOTHY J., J.C.L., The *Septimae Manus* Witness.

256. MAROSITZ, REV. JOSEPH J., M.S.C., J.C.L., Obligations and Privileges of Religious Promoted to the Episcopal or Cardinalitial Dignities.

257. MURPHY, REV. FRANCIS J., A.B., J.C.L., Legislative Powers of the Provincial Council.

258. O'BRIEN, REV. ROMAEUS W., O. Carm., J.C.L., The Provincial Superior in Religious Orders of Men.

259. PFALLER, REV. BENEDICT A., O.S.B., J.C.L., The *Ipso facto* Effected Dismissal of Religious.

260. POPEK, REV. ALPHONSE S., M.A., J.C.L., The Rights and Obligations of Metropolitans.

261. RISTUCCIA, REV. BERNARD J., C.M., J.C.L., Quasi-Religious.

262. SONNTAG, REV. NATHANIEL L., O.F.M. Cap., J.C.L., Censorship of Special Classes of Books.

263. STADLER, REV. JOSEPH N., J.C.L., Frequent Holy Communion.

264. SZAL, REV. IGNATIUS J., J.C.L., The Communication of Catholics with Schismatics.

265. WAGNER, REV. URBAN S., O.F.M. Conv., J.C.L., Parochial Substitute Vicars and Supplying Priests.

www.ingramcontent.com/pod-product-compliance
Lightning Source LLC
LaVergne TN
LVHW050226080826
844660LV00012B/478

* 9 7 8 0 8 1 3 2 2 4 3 5 0 *